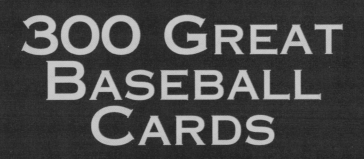

300 GREAT BASEBALL CARDS

of the 20th Century

———

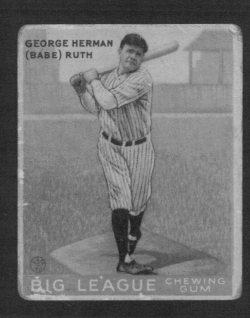

GEORGE HERMAN
(BABE) RUTH

BIG LEAGUE CHEWING GUM

A HISTORICAL TRIBUTE BY THE HOBBY'S MOST RELIED UPON SOURCE

MIKE PAYNE

and the Staff of Beckett Baseball Card Monthly

ACKNOWLEDGEMENTS

No book this size can be done without assistance, and I certainly had plenty of that. Special thanks to Rich Klein of Beckett Publications for his assistance and his mind for detail; Wayne Grove, for use of his personal card collection; Levi Bleam of 707 Sportscards in Plumsteadville, Pa.; Chipper Jones; Steve Hunt; Mike Jaspersen; Craig Ferris; Orve Johansson of The Baseball Card Company in Largo, Fla.; Galen and Tim Wilde of Shiretown Coins in Houlton, Maine; art director Carol Trammel; Len Shelton; Randall Calvert; Wayne Varner's Shoebox Cards of Zelienople, Pa.; associate editor Joel Brown; and finally, to my own team at home — Jodi, Jesse, Ryan and Carly — who make me feel like an all-star every time I walk through the door.

    — Mike Payne

Published by
Beckett Publications
15850 Dallas Parkway
Dallas, Texas 75248

ISBN: 1-887432-80-9
Beckett® is a registered trademark of Beckett Publications. This book is not licensed, authorized or endorsed by any individual, player, league or players association.

First Edition: September 1999
Beckett Corporate Sales and Information
(972) 991-6657

The values reported within this book pertain to the most commonly traded top grade for each era. Those grades and eras are as follows:

Pre-War (1947–back)
Excellent Mint (ExMt)
Typical conditions could include centering of 70/30 or better, slightly fuzzy corners, very minor paper discoloration, noticeable print spots or minor color or focus imperfections.

1948-1973
Near Mint (NM)
Typical conditions could include centering of 65/35 or better, a slight touch of wear on a few corners or print spots.

1974-1987
Near Mint/Mint (NmMt)
Typical conditions could include centering of 60/40 or better, a speck of wear on a few corners or a few small print spots.

1988 to Present
Mint
Typical conditions could include centering of 55/45 or better, four sharp corners (a tiny speck of wear seen under intense scrutiny is allowed) or one minor print spot.

FOREWORD

A ny chance you have to impress the younger generation, you need to take advantage of it. Baseball has been in trouble in years past, and I feel I am a spokesman and ambassador of the game. So if I can promote it and affect the life of a 10-year-old every once in awhile, I feel I'm doing my job.

Maybe I meet them and pass out some signed baseball cards, and all of a sudden they start following the game on a daily basis. Soon they're studying it and playing it, and then they're wanting to get better. Then all of a sudden they're knocking on the doorstep.

I never really thought about it until recently, but I run into fans every once in a while who can recite every high school statistic, every minor league honor, I ever had. That's getting into it. Those are the die-hard fans. That comes from cards.

I think baseball cards can affect the game. Fans are the ones who ultimately pay our salary, and the baseball card is one thing that promotes the game. It's fun to sit with buddies and trade out cards. It's fun to look at statistics. I know I used to do it all the time — look at the back of those cards and see which year was Mike Schmidt's career year or look and see which year Tony Gwynn had his most hits in a season. That luster hasn't left people around the country. True baseball lovers will always be baseball card lovers. They'll always be fascinated by statistics and the personalities behind those statistics.

The guy I really got into was Mickey Mantle. I have a lot of Mickey Mantle stuff. My dad was a huge Mickey Mantle fan, so I became a fan. That's why I became a switch hitter, because Mickey Mantle was a switch hitter.

I remember there was a lady whose husband played for the old Boston Braves, and she had a bunch of memorabilia. Well, she was having a yard sale, and she called my father. It turns out she had a plaque with four Mickey Mantle rookie cards on it. She also had a signed Mickey Mantle action shot with the date and everything on it. Knowing that I was a Mickey Mantle buff, my father gave them to me, so I have quite a collection.

I did a card show with Mantle in 1992. Getting to meet him was, maybe, one of the single greatest days in my life. It was really awkward, because I'm not a guy to get tongue-tied all that much. But the night before, I found myself standing in front of the mirror and rehearsing what I'd say to the guy. Then, when the time came, I basically froze. I couldn't say a word. That's the kind of presence, the kind of aura, Mickey Mantle had about him. He was very intimidating. He was a legend in the greatest sports town in America. What other way can you explain it?

I was a little bit embarrassed. He probably walked away saying, "Who's this guy who can't say a word to me?" But he extended me a lot of courtesy because of who I was, and it really blew me away. He signed a couple of baseballs for me on the sweet spot. I will be a Mickey Mantle collector until the day I die.

To be honest, I don't collect a lot of my own stuff. I do keep things that people give me, but the cards that the companies give me throughout the course of the year — the Topps cards, the Fleer cards, etc. — I basically use to give away. At Halloween, for instance, when kids come to my house I give them away. Or maybe I'll give cards to a friend of a friend of the family. It goes right on down the line. My parents ask me for cards to give to kids around town, and friends come to me and ask to sign 25 cards or so to give to kids in their town.

But I understand. I probably couldn't tell you which cards are the best ones to get, which cards are 50 cents or $500, but I know that I'm a historian, and I like to read up on the game. And when I come across anything with Ty Cobb, Babe Ruth, Joe D., Ted Williams, Stan the Man — anything with any of the great players' names on it — I want it.

And I think it's cool to be able to walk down into my basement every now and then just to see all of the stuff I've been able to collect.

Chipper Jones

Chipper Jones

Braves third baseman Chipper Jones, the first overall pick by Atlanta in the 1990 amateur draft, has two cards on the list of 300 Great Baseball Cards: his 1991 Bowman #569 and his 1991 Topps #333. Jones was interviewed for this foreword by Beckett associate editor Joel Brown.

INTRODUCTION

———✦———

Three hundred great cards. That's what this book is about.

Three hundred cards that have stood out from the tens of thousands produced in the past 100 years. Three hundred cards of stars, superstars and even a couple ordinary players who simply found their Warholian 15 minutes of fame.

Each of the cards on these pages tells a story. Sometimes it's with the words that accompany the card; sometimes it's the card itself that speaks volumes. But each of the 300 has something to say about the player pictured, the era of the time or the background of the card.

We've listed market values with the cards, but it would be a mistake to judge the greatness of a card purely on its monetary value while dismissing on-field contributions of the player, his personality and, of course, history. For it's history that makes baseball such a great game, and baseball cards such a significant part of society. Only in America can Mark McGwire knock Monica Lewinsky off the front page. And only in America can a Mark McGwire 1985 Topps Rookie Card go from being a pretty good card of a pretty good player to a historical card of a historical player, all in a matter of months.

The beauty of baseball cards is that you don't have to have played the game to collect the men who do play the game. Being a collector isn't an exclusive fraternity. Anyone with a little pocket change is in.

The following pages illustrate a group of cards and players who have made their marks on the collecting world and on the game of baseball. It's not a list of the most expensive cards or the all-time greatest cards ever produced. No, that would have left out too many of the other deserving cards, cards that are great in a non-monetary, non-scarce way.

The title says it all: "300 Great Baseball Cards of the 20th Century."

That's what this book is all about.

Mike Payne

Mike Payne

CHRISTY MATHEWSON

THE POLO GROUNDS

With the arrival of the 20th century, baseball cards became a premium in packs of cigarettes as well as in packages of caramels. The attraction of the game — Base Ball as it was written at the time — helped fuel interest in the small ballplayer images.

In 1901, the United States lost President William McKinley to an assassination. Theodore Roosevelt was inaugurated as the 26th President of the United States, and the country forged ahead into the decade. Orville Wright made the first successful flight in a self-propelled airplane, the New York City subway system opened, the Ford Motor Company produced the first Model-T automobile and Sigmund Freud published "The Interpretation of Dreams."

1900
1909

In baseball, the American League was formed in 1901 to take on the National League in many eastern cities. The first World Series was played in 1903, and Honus Wagner of the Pittsburgh Pirates and Ty Cobb of the Detroit Tigers were the hitting heroes of the decade. Christy Mathewson, who won three games and hurled 27 shutout innings for the New York Giants in the 1905 World Series, was one of the game's biggest stars and one of the first true role models.

Near the end of the decade came the release of a landmark set: the T206 tobacco set. It would prove to be one of the most important sets ever produced.

HONUS WAGNER

1909 T204 RAMLY WALTER JOHNSON

This is a great tobacco card showing The Big Train in the prime of his youth. The Ramly set is one of the key sets of the T-series cards (tobacco cards). Johnson's stare is the last thing batters of his era saw before the blur of a blazing fastball. Note to Hollywood: Should you ever have a need for a Johnson lookalike for "The Walter Johnson Story," give Robin Williams a call.

$2,250–$4,500

1909–11 T206 TY COBB (GREEN BACKGROUND)

The author chose his words very carefully: "Ty Cobb," biographer Charles Alexander once said during an interview, "was not a . . . *pleasant* man." Those who endured Cobb's wrath (including a verbal fan in New York who was pummeled by Cobb) and sharpened spikes-high slides, probably would not disagree. But Cobb left a legacy in baseball that reached far beyond the brawling, cursing and general unpleasantness. It stretched to the record books, where Cobb saw hitting as a science and he was the professor. Few could argue, even if they dared. This Cobb card is one of four in the T206 set, and is the most popular, because it appears to be available in lesser quantities than the other three.

$1,250–$2,500

1909–11 T206 EDDIE PLANK

This Plank card is among the scarcer cards in the T206 set, which just happens to be the King of the Hill and Mack Daddy of all tobacco sets. It's not that Eddie was a short print or anything like that — we're not even sure the world had heard of short prints way back then — but rather it's believed that most of the Plank cards were damaged from a faulty printing plate, so most of the cards were destroyed or pitched, or both.

$12,500–$25,000

1909–11 T206 Cy Young

Denton True "Cy" Young was so good, a pitching award was named after him. Only the Denton True part was left off. Of course, any pitcher who racks up 511 career victories should, indeed, have an award named after him, if not a candy bar. This is one of three Cy Young cards in the T206 set, and one of the few issued during Young's playing career.

$350–$700

1909–11 T206 Sherry Magee

One of the great error cards of our time, and certainly one of the most expensive, is this card of Sherwood Robert "Sherry" Magee in which the player's name is misspelled "Magie" and then corrected very early in the print run. And if you wonder why the spelling of a seemingly obscure player such as Magee was changed by the printers, look no further than his 1910 stats in which he led the NL in batting average, slugging average, runs and RBI. He also reeled off 49 stolen bases that season. No wonder they wanted to get the name right; the guy was a player.

$3,400–$6,800

1909–11 T206 HONUS WAGNER

Now, here's a card you might have heard of. *Everybody* has heard of this card. It's the Holy Grail of the card-collecting hobby. It's Boardwalk in a sea of Mediterranean Avenues. Reports on how many Wagner cards exist vary, but somewhere between 50–100 seems to be a solid estimate. For years it was thought that Wagner had his card pulled because he had an aversion to tobacco products. That's not entirely true. While Wagner wasn't keen on smoking cigarettes and perhaps was uncomfortable with kids buying cigarettes to get his card, he did enjoy a wad of chewing tobacco once in awhile. Indeed, in recent years it's been suggested — by a Wagner family member, in fact — that it was a money squabble that prompted the player to order his card pulled from distribution very early in the process. One of the few cards that did make it into circulation sold for a sports-card record $640,500 in auction in 1996.

$112,500–$225,000

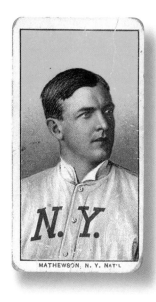

1909–11 T206 CHRISTY MATHEWSON (PORTRAIT)

Christy (short for Christopher) Mathewson was a huge star long before the era of mass-media-created superstars.
Tall with blue eyes and a Bucknell education, he was almost too good to be true. He was Cal Ripken long before Cal Ripken. There was a sense of fairness to Mathewson, and his clean lifestyle was the talk of the league back in the day. More important than anything else, though, was the fact that Matty could pitch. His performance in the 1905 World Series still ranks as one of the finest in Series history: three complete game victories over the Philadelphia Athletics as the Giants won the Series in five games. In that Series, Mathewson struck out 18 and walked just one in 27 innings. Mathewson is featured on three cards in the T206 set, but this one captures the essence of one of the game's — and nation's — first athletic superstars.

$500–$1,000

1910
1919

JOE JACKSON

T his was a difficult decade for the country, which saw catastrophe and war. The Titanic sunk during her maiden voyage in 1912, sinking the world's feeling of invincibility with it. Three years later, a German submarine torpedoed the British liner Lusitania, killing 124 Americans on board.

Within two years of the Lusitania incident, the United States had declared war on Germany, and World War I was underway.

But there were some positives. The first film studio was established in Hollywood, Willis Carrier designed the first air conditioning system, and the Panama Canal, linking the Atlantic and Pacific Oceans, was completed.

COMISKEY PARK

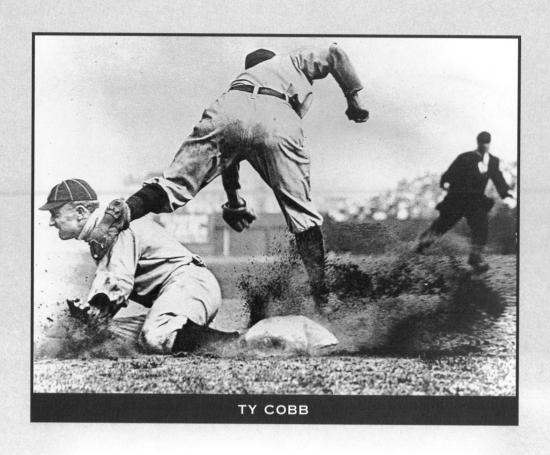

TY COBB

The baseball world was introduced to Red Sox pitcher George Herman "Babe" Ruth and got to know a sweet-swinging lefthander with the Athletics, Indians and White Sox known as "Shoeless" Joe Jackson. By the end of the decade, Jackson and seven of his White Sox teammates would be infamous for their parts in allegedly "fixing" the 1919 World Series to collect money from gamblers.

Baseball cards got better during the decade. While cigarette and caramel cards were still widely produced and distributed, other companies, such as Cracker Jack and The Sporting News, produced popular sets.

1911 T205
GOLD BORDERS
JOE TINKER

1911 T205
GOLD BORDERS
JOHNNY EVERS

These are the saddest of possible words
  Tinker to Evers to Chance
Trio of Bear Cubs and fleeter than birds
  Tinker to Evers to Chance
Ruthlessly pricking our gonfalon bubble
Making a Giant hit into a double —
Words that are weighty with nothing but
  trouble —
  Tinker to Evers to
  Chance
— FRANKLIN P. ADAMS

$125–$250

1911 T205
GOLD BORDERS
FRANK CHANCE

1912 T202 HASSAN CIGARETTES TRIPLE FOLDER CHARLES O'LEARY/TY COBB

The center folder in most of the Hassan Triple Folders adds a great deal of historical significance to these cards. This is one of the better examples, picturing Ty Cobb sliding into third base. Even through the graininess of the old photo, the intensity and desire of Cobb is crystal clear.

$700–$1,400

1912 T207 TRIS SPEAKER

The brown background of this card helps "The Gray Eagle" look almost regal. A man whose dying words were "I am Tris Speaker" will forever be remembered as a player who covered as much ground in the outfield as anyone at anytime. Speaker played a shallow center field, robbing batters of bloop hits that would fall in front of other outfielders. He also was able to race back and haul in even the deepest of shots. Along with his defense came the ability to hit, and hit he did, finishing his career with more than 3,500 hits and a lifetime .345 average.

$600–$1,200

1913 TOM BARKER BASEBALL GAME JOE JACKSON

From 1911 through 1913, Joe Jackson — with all due respect to Ty Cobb — might have been the best hitter in baseball. In '11, he batted .408, then followed it up with a .395 mark in '12 and .373 in '13. He ripped an amazing 26 triples in 1912, and led the league in hits in both '12 and '13. Maybe Joe actually was onto something when he would collect all of his bats and take them home with him to South Carolina after the Indians' season ended each year. The way Joe saw it, bats were like people, and they didn't like cold weather.

$250–$500

1912 T207 BUCK WEAVER

Weaver, one of the Eight Men Out on the Chicago Black Sox, is a sad figure in the history of the game. Weaver's only crime in baseball was his attendance in a meeting with seven teammates, in which accepting money from gamblers — in exchange for purposely losing games in the 1919 World Series — was discussed. But let the record speak for itself: Buck Weaver batted .324 with 11 hits, including five for extra bases in that Series, and did not commit an error at third base in 27 attempts. It's documented that Weaver never asked for, nor received, any dirty money. Not a cent. Still, Judge Kenesaw Mountain Landis banned him from baseball with the others, for simply failing to report what he heard. For years, Weaver petitioned the commissioner's office for reinstatement, but it was never granted. Weaver maintained his innocence up until his death in 1956 of heart failure. Or, perhaps, it was from a broken heart.

$300–$600

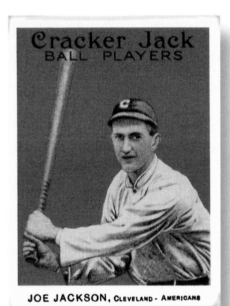

1914 CRACKER JACK JOE JACKSON #103

In the past 15 years, Joe Jackson's life has taken on almost mythical proportions. The release of "Eight Men Out" and "Field of Dreams" introduced a whole new generation to "Shoeless" Joe Jackson, clearly one of the game's greatest hitters. But his career lasted such a short time. Jackson was banned from baseball for his uncertain role in the 1919 Black Sox scandal. It's believed by some that Jackson, not a finely-educated man, simply got caught up in something he didn't understand when he accepted an invitation for $5,000 for a role in "throwing" the Series. But in the Series, Joe played like Joe always played. And like teammate Buck Weaver, Jackson played hard in the Series. Jackson batted .375 (12-for-32) with a home run and six RBI. He also did not commit an error in the outfield in 17 chances. You be the judge.

$4,000–$8,000

1915 SPORTING NEWS BABE RUTH M101-5

Here's all you really need to know about this card: It's the Babe Ruth Rookie Card. There have been other items that have popped up with pictures of the young Bambino — a schedule for one thing — but not an actual card. That's where this issue comes in. This is the first card The Babe ever appeared on, and chances are, back in 1915 few people cared. The previous season, which was Ruth's first in the major leagues, he hardly stood out, walking seven and striking out three in 21 innings. Worse, he didn't appear to be much of a hitter, either. He batted .200 that first season, and did not hit a home run. So you can imagine why this card might have generated a collective yawn back in its day. My, how things have changed.

$3,000–$6,000

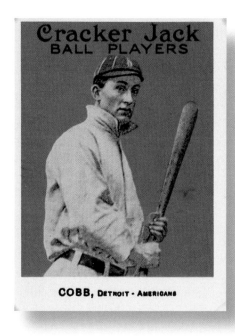

1914 CRACKER JACK TY COBB #30

When all was said and done, Ty Cobb — The Georgia Peach — received 222 of a possible 226 votes for the first-ever Hall of Fame induction in 1936, leading all candidates. At the time, it spoke volumes to his career on the field. It still does today.

$3,000–$6,000

1920
1929

The Roaring Twenties opened with baseball fans witnessing Babe Ruth, in his first season as a New York Yankee in 1920, shatter the home run record he had set just one year before. Ruth's total of 54 home runs was an astounding 25 homers more than he had slugged in 1919, his final season with Boston. The next season, 1921, he slugged 59 homers. It marked the arrival of the Sultan of Swat, and helped — along with the Ruth- and Lou Gehrig-led Murderer's Row Yankees of 1927 — provide Yankee Stadium (built in 1923) with the unofficial name of The House that Ruth Built.

Naturally, baseball cards picturing The Bambino were as popular with fans as The Babe himself. From the W-516 strip cards that featured little more than a crude rendering of the player depicted, to various caramel cards of the decade, Ruth cards were in demand. A six-card set

BABE RUTH

YANKEE STADIUM

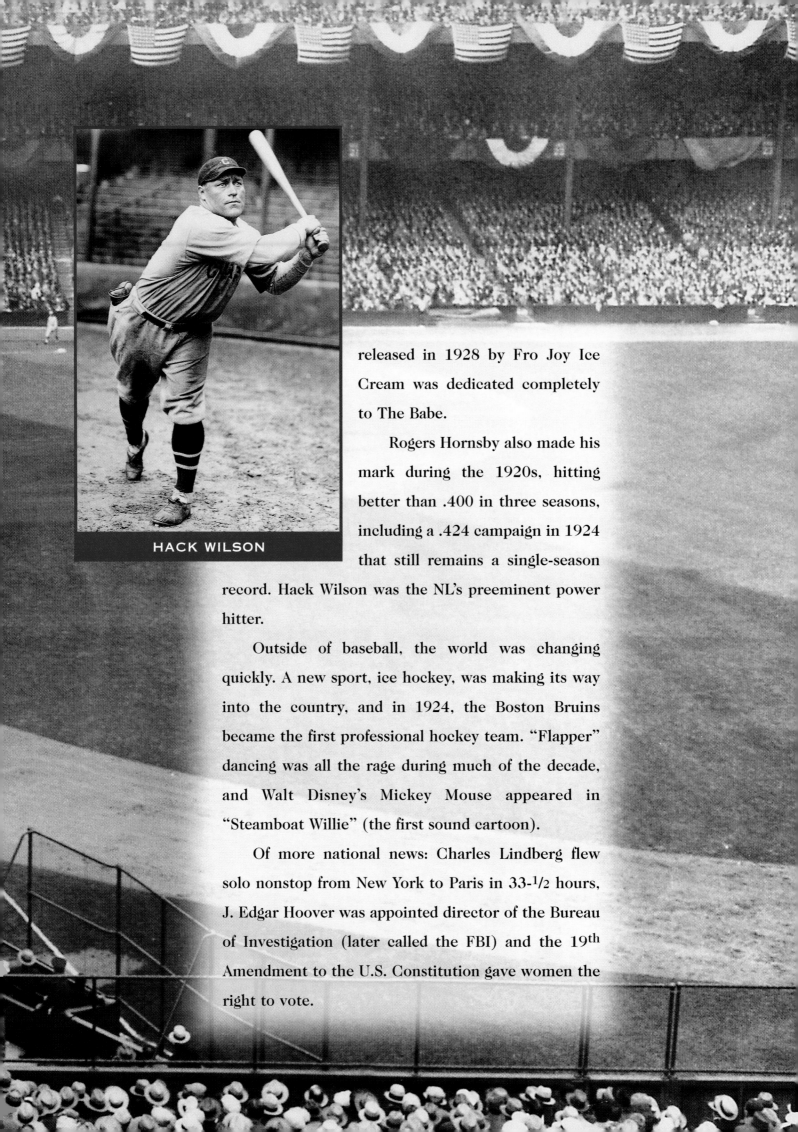

HACK WILSON

released in 1928 by Fro Joy Ice Cream was dedicated completely to The Babe.

Rogers Hornsby also made his mark during the 1920s, hitting better than .400 in three seasons, including a .424 campaign in 1924 that still remains a single-season record. Hack Wilson was the NL's preeminent power hitter.

Outside of baseball, the world was changing quickly. A new sport, ice hockey, was making its way into the country, and in 1924, the Boston Bruins became the first professional hockey team. "Flapper" dancing was all the rage during much of the decade, and Walt Disney's Mickey Mouse appeared in "Steamboat Willie" (the first sound cartoon).

Of more national news: Charles Lindberg flew solo nonstop from New York to Paris in 33-1/2 hours, J. Edgar Hoover was appointed director of the Bureau of Investigation (later called the FBI) and the 19th Amendment to the U.S. Constitution gave women the right to vote.

Ruth is a Crack Fielder

The Big Leagues cannot boast a surer fielder than the Home Run King. The photograph shows him scooping up a liner preparatory to a double play that retired the opposing team and put the game on ice for the World's Champions.

1928 F52 FRO JOY BABE RUTH "RUTH IS A CRACK FIELDER"

All the home runs and bigger-than-life personality tend to obscure the fact that The Sultan of Swat was also a pretty decent outfielder. This Fro Joy card is from a six-card set dedicated to Ruth. That's the good news. The bad news is the set itself is one of the most commonly illegally reprinted sets from the era.

$50–$100

BABE RUTH
OUTFIELD, NEW YORK AMERICANS

1921 NEILSON'S CHOCOLATE BABE RUTH #37

In 1921, about the time our nation's youth was looking at this card and thinking "cool," (or whatever it was kids thought in those days) the Great Bambino was en route to 59 home runs (second most in his career) and 177 RBI (most in his career). This is one of The Babe's first Yankees cards, and it's a beauty.

$900–$1,800

ROGERS HORNSBY
SECOND BASE, ST. LOUIS NATIONALS

1921 NEILSON'S CHOCOLATE ROGERS HORNSBY #81

Considered by many to be the greatest right-handed hitter of all-time, Hornsby finished his 23-year major-league career with a .358 average that included three complete seasons above the .400 mark. His .424 average in 1924 is still a record. The Rajah is one of the big four of the 120-card Neilson's set, joining Babe Ruth, Ty Cobb and Walter Johnson as the elite names.

$125–$250

DIZZY DEAN

Even with the country mired in The Great Depression during the 1930s, baseball cards enjoyed a great revival during the decade brought on by some great sets such as the U.S. Caramel Company's 1932 set, and the Goudey releases of 1933 and 1934 that featured, among others, Babe Ruth and Lou Gehrig.

The Goudey cards, along with others sets such as National Chicle's Diamond Stars and the Delong and Sport Kings sets of 1933, were issued with bubble gum which would become a common form of card distribution for the next 50-plus years.

In 1933, Franklin D. Roosevelt was inaugurated as the 32nd President of the United States, and a year later Adolf Hitler became the leader of Germany. The decade of the '30s also saw the introduction of the board game Monopoly, The Star Spangled Banner was named the U.S. National Anthem, the German airship Hindenburg was destroyed by fire during a flight over Lakehurst, N.J., Orson Welles' radio broadcast of "War of the Worlds" scared just about everyone, and two

WRIGLEY FIELD

1930
1939

memorable films — "The Wizard of Oz" and "Gone With the Wind" — were released in 1939.

On the ball field, the decade opened with Hack Wilson's 191 RBI in 1930, and a few years later the first major league All-Star Game was introduced and played in Chicago. In St. Louis, Dizzy Dean and the Gas House Gang reigned. Hank Greenberg and Jimmie Foxx both turned in 58 home run seasons during the 1930s. And before the decade ended, Joe DiMaggio and Ted Williams had arrived in the major leagues and Lou Gehrig was telling the world that, although dying of amyotrophic lateral sclerosis, he was "the luckiest man on the face of the earth."

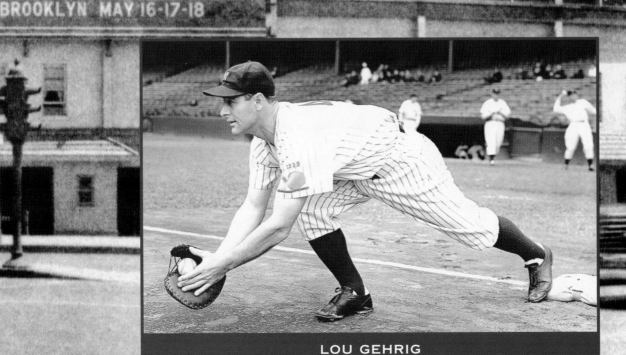

LOU GEHRIG

1933 DELONG LOU GEHRIG #7

The Iron Horse, as many remember him: bigger than life. This card was pulled from a Delong Gum pack. Alas, Delong produced just one 24-card set.

$1,750–$3,500

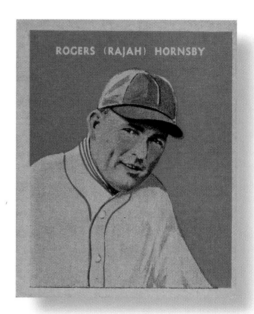

1932 U.S. CARAMEL ROGERS HORNSBY #11

As good as he was at hitting a baseball as a player, as a manager, The Rajah sometimes whiffed at public relations. Hornsby lacked one little detail: tact. Hornsby would berate anyone he felt needed it, from management types to players. Indeed, Hornsby's verbal outbursts are legendary and lingered with those at the receiving end. In the film "A League of Their Own," fictional manager Jimmy Dugan screams at one of his female players about the sense of throwing home with a two-run lead. When the girl breaks into tears, Dugan goes into this fine tirade: "Rogers Hornsby was my manager, and he called me a talking pile of pink [stuff]. And that's after my parents had driven all the way down from Michigan to watch me play. But did I cry? No! No! And you know why? Because there's no crying. There's no crying in baseball." Ah . . . even Hollywood remembers The Rajah.

$200–$400

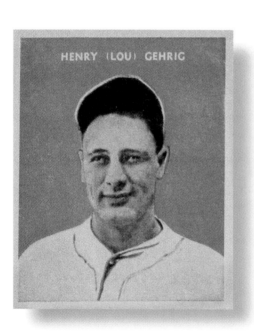

1932 U.S. CARAMEL LOU GEHRIG #26

One of the few cards that identifies The Iron Horse by his real name, "Henry." If he hadn't used part of his middle name (Louis), the record books could have easily shown that it was Babe Ruth and Hank Gehrig who were at the heart of Murderer's Row.

$500–$1,000

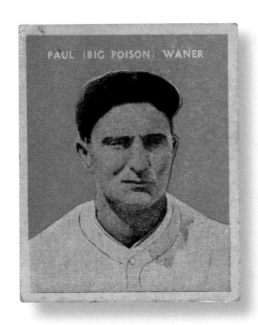
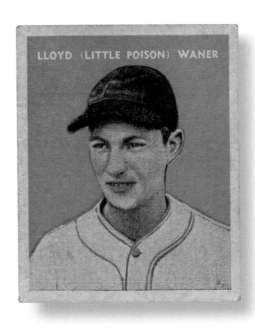

1932 U.S. CARAMEL PAUL (BIG POISON) WANER #2
1932 U.S. CARAMEL LLOYD (LITTLE POISON) WANER #13

Pick your Poison. For 14 years, the Waner brothers played together in the
Pittsburgh Pirates outfield. Paul was three years older; Lloyd was three steps
faster. Both hit their way to the Hall of Fame, and both are part of the 1932
U.S. Caramel set, one of the last caramel sets released before the bubble
gum and baseball card marriage emerged.

$150–$350

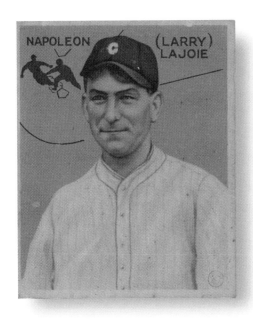

1933 GOUDEY NAPOLEON (LARRY) LAJOIE #106

Simply one of the greatest cards of all
time, and one of the toughest to find in
any condition. Lajoie became the sixth
player elected to the Hall of Fame, yet
he couldn't find his way into the 1933
Goudey set . . . until 1934. Many kids
and collectors just did not realize there
was no card #106 in their '33 sets.
Once they did — and Goudey realized
its mistake — the company printed the
Lajoie card and sent it to any collector
requesting one. Subsequently, many of
the Lajoie cards in circulation carry
faint paper clip indentations because
that's how they were sent to collectors. The Lajoie cards not sent to
collectors, presumably were destroyed, leaving an undetermined
amount in circulation. But longtime collectors and dealers will tell
you, there aren't many copies out there. Not many at all.

$15,000–$30,000

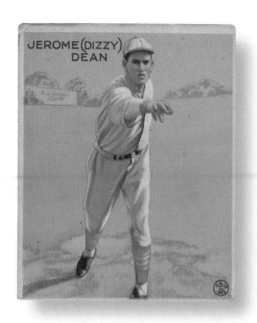

1933 GOUDEY DIZZY DEAN #223

"X-rays on Dizzy's head show nothing." While Dean carried the reputation as a country bumpkin, he actually was one of the shrewdest and best pitchers in the National League during the 1930s. While a member of the St. Louis Cardinals' Gas House Gang, Dean was the last National League pitcher to win 30 games in a season, accomplishing that feat just one year after the release of this card.

$300–$600

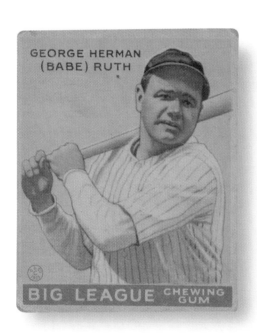

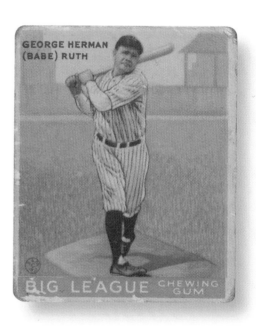

1933 GOUDEY BABE RUTH #53

The Goudey Gum Company knew a good thing when it saw it. And the company saw Babe Ruth, signed on the line that is dotted, to appear in Goudey sets. And so the good folks at Goudey made sure the buyers of Goudey gum packs saw The Babe as well — four times to be exact. You can never get enough of a good thing.

$2,000–$4,000

1933 GOUDEY BABE RUTH #144

This card is the only double print of the group of four Ruths. The Babe's four cards in the set are more than any other player's cards. Some of the other stars of the day, including Lou Gehrig, were featured on two cards. This double print allowed more Ruth cards to circulate to kids.

$1,500–$3,000

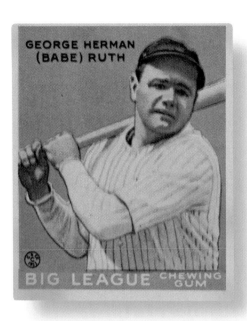

1933 GOUDEY BABE RUTH #149

It was Waite Hoyt, Hall of Fame pitcher and former Yankees teammate of Ruth, who said, "Every big league player and his wife should teach their children to pray, 'God bless Mommy, God bless Daddy and God bless Babe Ruth.'"

Amen.

$2,000–$4,000

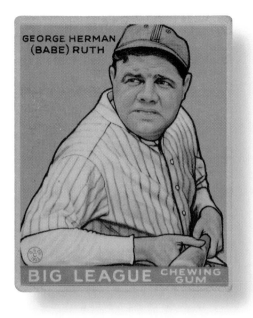

1933 GOUDEY BABE RUTH #181

Ruth's final pitching performance came during the same season as this card's release: 1933. The Babe, then 38 and gaining weight, took the mound for one start (even though he had long since given up pitching) and hurled a complete-game, nine-inning victory. He walked three and did not strike out a batter. It would be the last time the game's greatest slugger ever took the mound.

$2,000–$4,000

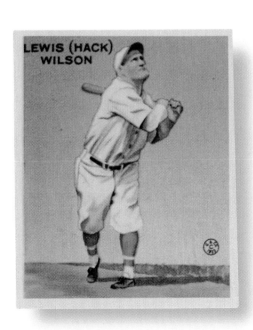

1933 GOUDEY HACK WILSON #211

Hack Wilson was a big man. Heck, just look at the card front. That's an 18-20 collar if ever we saw one. In 1930, Wilson was a giant. Actually, he was a Cub, but he was a giant at the plate, setting an NL record of 56 home runs that stood until Mark McGwire's 70 homers in 1998. The other record Wilson set in '30 may never be approached, let alone broken: 191 RBI.

No, that's not a misprint.

$150–$300

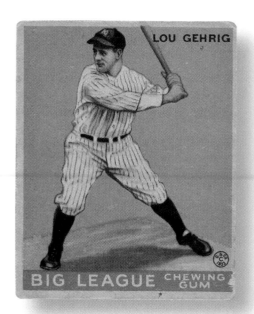

1933 GOUDEY LOU GEHRIG #92
1933 GOUDEY LOU GEHRIG #160

In case collectors missed Gehrig #92, there was always Gehrig #160 to grab. Both are among The Iron Horse's most collected cards. At the time these cards were released, Babe Ruth was still getting all the attention in New York and around the country. But Lou was close to supplanting The Babe as the most important and valuable Yankee in the lineup.

$1,250—$2,500

1934–36 DIAMOND STARS MICKEY COCHRANE #9

The National Chicle Company's Diamond Stars issue isn't Mickey Cochrane's first card, nor is it a particularly difficult card to find. But the clenched fist picture certainly does capture the spirit of the HOF catcher. Cochrane, dubbed "Black Mike" for his competitive and down-and-dirty mentality, helped the Tigers to the 1935 World Series title as a player-manager. Sadly, his career ended in 1937 when he was beaned in the skull by Yankees pitcher Bump Hadley. But Cochrane's toughness was never questioned in his career, and his play-hard inspiration led one Oklahoma father to name his son after Cochrane. That boy, Mickey Charles Mantle, turned out to be something of a player himself. But that's another story.

$90—$175

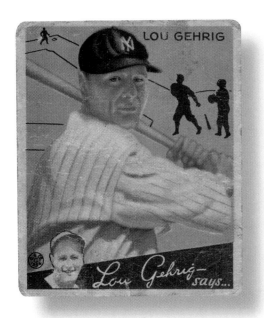

1934 GOUDEY LOU GEHRIG #61

In 1934, Lou Gehrig was credited with 579 at-bats. In those plate appearances he: (1) whacked 49 home runs; (2) collected 165 RBI; (3) drilled 40 doubles; (4) and led the league with a .363 average. What's even more impressive is that he struck out just a measly 31 times. Oh yeah, he also appeared at shortstop in one game. What a guy.

$1,350–$2,700

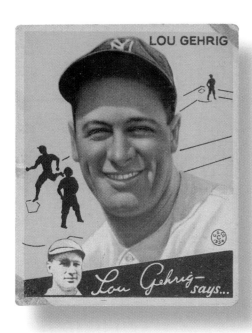

1934 GOUDEY LOU GEHRIG #37

The Goudey Gum Company was onto something in 1934 when the company chose Gehrig to promote its baseball card set. Gehrig, after all, was a mother's dream. He loved his wife, respected his mama and played a mean game of ball. And while Babe Ruth is mysteriously missing from this set, Gehrig has two cards in the 98-card offering. A picture of The Iron Horse can also be found on the fronts of 84 cards in the set, along with the words "Lou Gehrig says . . ." It was a superstar pitch about 60 years before superstar pitches came into vogue.

$1,350–$2,700

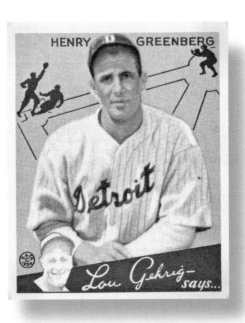

1934 GOUDEY HANK GREENBERG #62

Hank Greenberg might have been a New York Yankee had it not been for one thing: a fellow by the name of Gehrig. Oh, Hank wanted to be a Yankee. He grew up in the Bronx and followed the exploits of Ruth, Gehrig and crew, but Greenberg knew his position was first base. And first base for the Yankees was a done deal. But the Yankees still offered him a lucrative contract. He declined, as he also did with an offer from the Washington Senators, and instead signed with the Detroit Tigers. This card was released just one year after his call-up to the big leagues, and just two years before his first AL MVP Award (he won two) with 36 HR and 170 RBI. In 1937, he collected 183 RBI — still third best ever. Clearly, the Yankees' loss was the Tigers' gain.

$190–$375

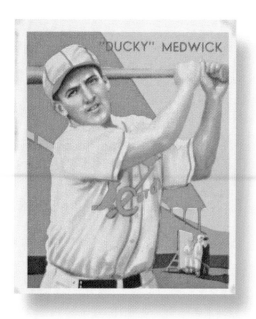

1934–36 Diamond Stars "Ducky" Medwick #66

Joe Medwick had two nicknames as a pro ballplayer, Ducky — which he wasn't particularly enamored with — and Muscles, which he could live with. To the public, however, it was Ducky. And so it was with the National Chicle Company, who even left off the "Joe" on the front of Medwick's Diamond Stars card in favor of the straight "Ducky." Medwick, recognized as one of the fiercest competitors of his era, won the NL's last Triple Crown in 1937 and was named NL MVP the same season. That's hardly anything to quack at.

$75–$150

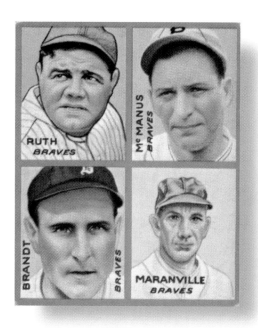

1935 Goudey Puzzle Backs Ruth/McManus/Brandt/Maranville

In one of The Babe's last cards as a player, he shares cardboard space with three Boston Braves teammates — yep, Boston Braves — including HOFer Rabbit Maranville. Ruth played 28 games with the Braves in '35, hitting the final six home runs of his career. But while this card reads "Braves," the Bambino still appears to be wearing Yankee pinstripes in the picture. And that's how we remember him.

$500–$1,000

1936 World Wide Gum Joe DiMaggio #51

Here's one of the very first cards picturing Joe DiMaggio. So new was DiMaggio to the big leagues that the card back lists his nickname as "Deadpan Joe," not Joltin' Joe or The Yankee Clipper.

$1600–$3500

No. 42 CHARLIE GEHRINGER

JOE DI MAGGIO
Centre field, New York Yankees

1936 WORLD WIDE GUM CHARLIE GEHRINGER #42

"The Mechanical Man" did everything right, and he did everything right quietly. He arrived at the ballpark quietly, took the field quietly, played a flawless second base quietly, dressed and showered quietly and then went home quietly, without fanfare. About the only thing Chas. Gehringer did loudly was fashion a HOF career that included a .320 lifetime average and 2,839 hits. Gehringer was a polite and respectful man who did his job well day in and day out — mechanical, they called it — earning one of the most fitting nicknames ever bestowed upon a player.

$75–$150

1937 O-PEE-CHEE BATTER UP JOE DiMAGGIO #118

By the time our collector friends north of the border were seeing these O-Pee-Chee Batter Up Canadian issues for the first time, Joltin' Joe already was considered an up-and-coming superstar.

$2,250–$4,500

BOB FELLER, Indians

1938 GOUDEY HEADS UP BOB FELLER #288

Two versions of 1938 Goudey Heads Up exist for each player in the set. One version contains the large head and caricature body, and the other features the same design along with cartoon facts along the side of the card, such as this doozie on Feller's issue: "Bob's Fast One Is The Talk Of Baseball." This isn't Rapid Robert's first card, but it is one of his earliest cards and the first Feller you could have pulled out of a pack.

$350–$700

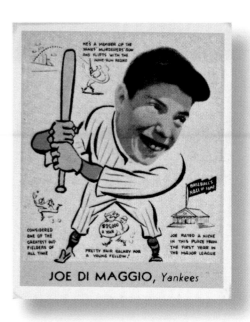

1938 Goudey Heads Up Joe DiMaggio #274

In 1938, Joltin' Joe DiMaggio had established himself as one of the game's brightest young stars. Having led the league in home runs (46) the previous season, he went on to hit .324-32-140 with 13 triples in '38, which happened to be Lou Gehrig's last full season with the Yanks. But for all of The Yankee Clipper's success, at no time that season did anyone, anywhere, even remotely suggest that Joe DiMaggio had a big head.

$2,250–$4,500

1939 Play Ball Joe DiMaggio #26

Gum Incorporated's '39 Play Ball set often is looked at as the start of the modern collecting era because of its post-Depression release. But that's not important. The important thing with this card is that it pictures Joe DiMaggio. That alone should be enough, but it also happens to have been issued in the same season that he captured the first of his three MVP awards. The historic significance just sort of drips right off it.

$1,250–$2,500

1939 Play Ball Ted Williams #92

What's this? Ted looks as if he's almost smiling in this picture, which clearly is before his battles with the press began. This card was issued in gum packs during The Splendid Splinter's rookie season, a season that saw the young Red Sox phenom hit .327 and lead the AL with 145 RBI. And as we all know now, there was so much more to come from this kid.

$1,250–$2,500

1940

1949

With the world situation growing increasingly unstable, it remained business as usual for the major leagues in the early part of the decade. Joe DiMaggio notched hits in 56 consecutive games in 1941, the same year Ted Williams hit .406. But by the end of the year, the Japanese had bombed Pearl Harbor, and America entered World War II. Within a year, the U.S. fleet defeated the Japanese at the Battle of Midway, a major turning point in the war in the Pacific.

Even the entertainment of the day centered on the country's war effort. Humphrey Bogart and Ingrid Bergman starred in "Casablanca," and actor Jimmy Cagney won an Academy Award for his work in the

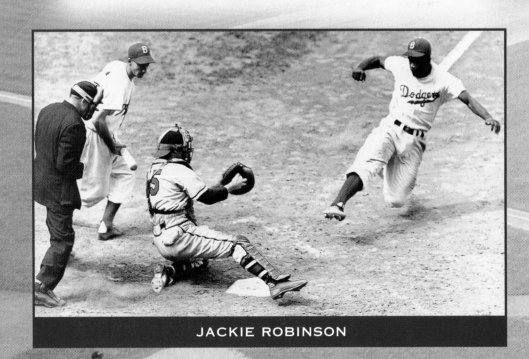

JACKIE ROBINSON

FENWAY PARK

film "Yankee Doodle Dandy." In 1945, the U.S. dropped atomic bombs on the Japanese cities of Hiroshima and Nagasaki, hastening the end of the war.

TED WILLIAMS

There were other headlines during the decade: The 10-team All-American Girls Baseball League drew nearly 1,000,000 fans in 1948, the United Nations was founded, Dr. Benjamin Spock published "The Commonsense Book of Baby and Child Care," American pilot Kenneth Arnold made the first alleged sighting of a UFO, and Jackie Robinson took the field as the first African-American in the major leagues.

The war curtailed a lot of the baseball card production — paper was needed for the war effort — but the decade did produce the classic 1941 Play Ball set, which was the final Play Ball set released. In 1948, the first Bowman set was issued, followed by the star-filled Leaf set in 1949. The Leaf set reintroduced collectors to colorized cards.

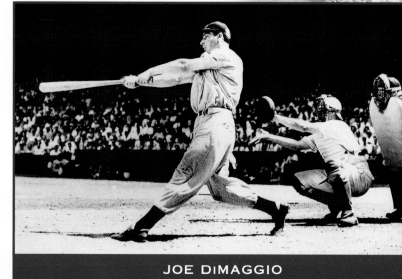

JOE DiMAGGIO

JOE DI MAGGIO

1940 PLAY BALL JOE DIMAGGIO #1

This is the card that led off the decently designed (but still black and white) 1940 Play Ball set from Gum, Inc. Being given top billing in the set was a sign that DiMaggio had made it big in baseball, and baseball cards.

$1,500–$3,000

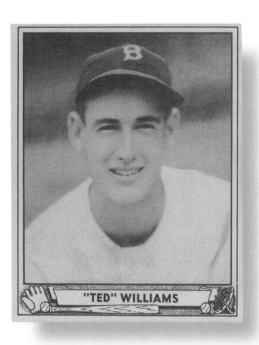

"TED" WILLIAMS

"PEE WEE" REESE

1941 PLAY BALL PEE WEE REESE #54

It's hard to believe that it's been almost 60 years since Pee Wee Reese broke in as a young shortstop with the Brooklyn Dodgers. Reese replaced Leo Durocher at shortstop for the Dodgers and would remain entrenched there until 1958. This card pictures an almost baby-faced Reese — Pee Wee, if you will — and was issued during the HOFer's rookie campaign.

$350–$700

1940 PLAY BALL TED WILLIAMS #27

The Red Sox were getting hammered by the Detroit Tigers on a warm August afternoon in 1940, and when the game reached the seventh inning, Boston manager Joe Cronin needed help. Cronin was looking for somebody — anybody, really — to volunteer for mop-up duty. Up stepped Ted Williams. The Kid had pitched a little at Hoover High in San Diego, so what the heck, right? In his two innings of work, arguably the best hitter ever to play the game allowed one run on three hits and — can you believe it — whiffed Rudy York with a curve. It would be Teddy Ballgame's only appearance on the mound in the big leagues.

$1,000–$2,000

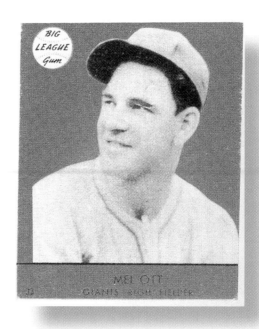

1941 PLAY BALL JOE DiMAGGIO #71

For two months during the 1941 season an entire nation was glued to the exploits of Joseph Paul DiMaggio, center fielder for the New York Yankees. On May 15, DiMaggio started his incredible string of hitting in 56 consecutive games before finally being held hitless by the Cleveland Indians on July 17. Kids who pulled this card from packs of gum that summer were sudden celebrities in their neighborhoods, and were treated with the same respect a lottery winner might receive from various hangers-on. Which, when you consider this card remains the most valuable in the entire set, seems appropriate to the lucky youth of '41.

$1,500–$3,000

1941 GOUDEY MEL OTT #33

Mel Ott never had one of those nifty nicknames of the era, like Rabbitt, Blondy or Cookie. Mel was about as good as it got for Melvin Ott of Gretna, La. Oh, there was the obligatory "Otter," but what's original about that? But shortly after Ott began driving balls out of the Polo Grounds with the strangest foot-in-the-bucket swing anyone had ever seen, he was given the name "Master Melvin," which would seem more appropriate for a Rap artist today than a home run slugger of the '30s and '40s. Ott went with it, however, becoming the first National Leaguer to reach the 500 home run mark. This card is from the last Goudey baseball set, a 33-card effort that features Ott and Carl Hubbell as the only big names.

$65–$125

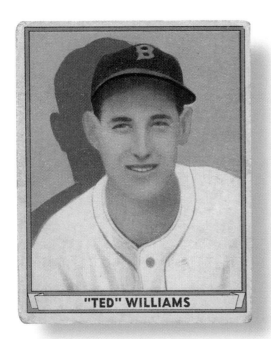

"TED" WILLIAMS

1941 Play Ball Ted Williams #14

If a guy hits .406, then he should be the hands-down, no-questions-asked winner of the MVP Award, right? Right. Only it didn't quite go that way for Ted Williams in 1941, his greatest season. You see, Joe DiMaggio just happened to string together his greatest season as well in '41, hitting in 56 straight games. And in the game of baseball, at least back in '41, 56 straight games trumped .406 and Joltin' Joe won the MVP. It wasn't a total loss for Ted. He looks great on this '41 Play Ball (just as he did on his '40 Play Ball card which featured the same photo of The Thumper) and he was given The Sporting News' award as baseball's Man of the Year, which isn't too shabby of a parting gift.

$1,000–$2,000

"CHARLEY" GEHRINGER

1941 Play Ball Charles Gehringer #19

Charlie Gehringer could hit (lifetime .320 average), but he separated himself from the pack with the glove. Seven times the second baseman led the AL in fielding average, including 1941 — the year this card was released. Gehringer played part of the '42 season, then retired at age 39. Among Gehringer's biggest fans as a player was his one-time manager with the Tigers: a fellow by the name of Ty Cobb. Yeah, Charlie was that good.

$50–$100

SPORT THRILLS
Highlights in the World of Sport

MOST DRAMATIC HOME RUN

1948 Swell Gum Sports Thrills #12

This card, from a set of 20 baseball thrills, honors Babe Ruth's alleged "called shot." Whether that really happened or not is up for debate, and probably will be forever. What we do know for sure is that this is a card picturing Ruth and Lou Gehrig. And that's Swell.

$100–$200

1948 BOWMAN YOGI BERRA #6

Yogi is one of those rare players whose outstanding play on the field was partially overshadowed by his incredibly entertaining personality away from it. Whether the famous Yogiisms are true or not is almost irrelevant. They're part of the Berra legend. Yet, in 1948, that legend hadn't been formed. He wasn't so much Yogi then as he was Larry. This Rookie Card started a run for Berra that saw him appear on a baseball card every year through 1964, a streak matched only by Warren Spahn.

$250–$450

1948 BOWMAN PHIL RIZZUTO #8

Whoop, Holy Cow! A fielding pose of the Scooter doing what he does best. Phil Rizzuto and Pee Wee Reese were two of a kind for the Yankees/Dodgers rivalry of the 1940s and '50s. Their careers mirrored each other, and the world saw their teams compete against each other in six World Series. The Scooter, like teammate Yogi Berra, became a legend almost as much for what he did off the field — Yankee broadcaster, Money Store pitchman and a key contributor on rock singer Meatloaf's "Paradise By The Dashboard Light" — as for what he did on it.

$175–$300

1948 BOWMAN STAN MUSIAL #36

Here's the card that introduced the world to Stan "The Man" Musial, the greatest player in Cardinals' history. The 1948 Bowman set represented the first major baseball card set of the post-war era.

$500–$800

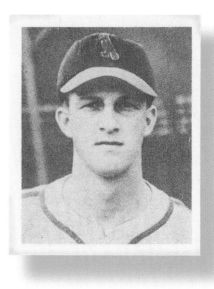

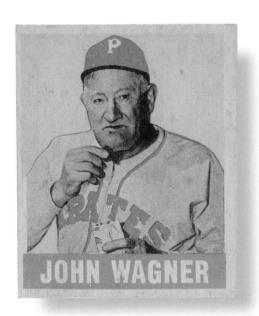

1949 LEAF JOHN WAGNER #70

This is Honus Wagner (real name John), as a coach with the Pittsburgh Pirates. So much for the Wagner dislikes tobacco theory. Actually, as noted elsewhere in this book, it was cigarette smoking that Honus — or John — didn't care for. Obviously, a wad of chaw here and there was fair game.

$200–$300

1949 LEAF BABE RUTH #3

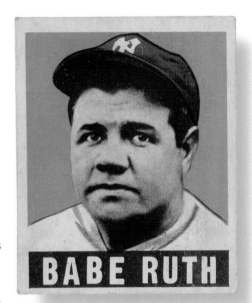

This card was released right about the time of Ruth's death of throat cancer, and is one of the more popular Ruth cards in the hobby. Ruth's death was a tremendous loss to baseball and the country as a whole, yet even in death The Bambino lived on with those whose lives he had touched. There's a well-documented story surrounding The Babe's funeral, which happened to fall on a particularly hot day. Joe Dugan, a former Yankees teammate of Ruth's and one of the pallbearers, felt the heat all too well.

"I'd give anything for a beer," Dugan told former Yankee Waite Hoyt.

Hoyt, a good friend of Ruth, never skipped a beat.

"So would The Babe," Hoyt replied.

$1,600–$2,500

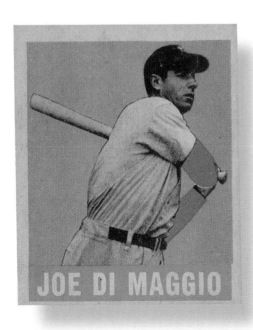

1949 LEAF JOE DiMAGGIO #1

The '49 season was a tough one for DiMaggio, who perhaps could see the end in sight. He missed the first 65 games of the season, but then returned to help the Yankees win the pennant — thanks in part to a .346 average in 76 games. DiMaggio would go on to play two more seasons before hanging it up for good. This is the first card in the first color set of the postwar issues.

$1,400–$2,200

1949 LEAF LEROY PAIGE #8

There's a story that has circulated around baseball circles for some time that provides a glimpse of the greatness of Satchel Paige. Brought to the Cleveland Indians in 1948 from the Negro Leagues, Paige was working out of the bullpen in an important game against the Yankees. At the time, the Yanks were challenging the Tribe for first place in the American League standings. With Cleveland nursing a slim lead in the ninth inning, the Yanks threatened with no outs and Phil Rizzuto leading off third base. The call came to the bullpen for Paige, and as he slowly walked to the mound Paige passed Rizzuto, looked at him and said, "Don't get nervous little man, you ain't goin' nowhere." He then retired the side on 10 pitches. This Rookie Card of Paige is a short print, and ranks right up there in value with Babe Ruth.

$1,500–$2,500

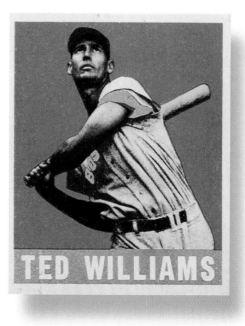

1949 LEAF STAN MUSIAL #4

Stan Musial's SABR (Society of American Baseball Research) profile reads "Expertise — Hitting a Baseball." It's kind of hard to argue with that.

$550–$850

1949 LEAF TED WILLIAMS #76

Ted displayed a little pop in '49, and if anyone thought his average would suffer if he hit home runs, they were quickly proven wrong. While finishing at .343, Williams led the American League with 43 home runs, 159 RBI, 39 doubles, 150 runs, 162 walks and a .650 slugging average. Splendid, indeed.

$500–$900

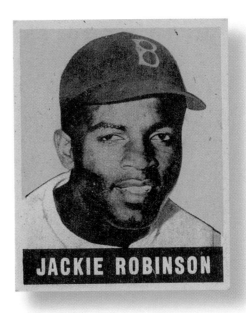

1949 Bowman Stan Musial #24

Stan the Man already was a star in 1949, and if a kid didn't want to be Ted Williams or Joe DiMaggio, then he wanted to be Stan Musial. This second-year Musial card shows The Man ready for action.

$300–$500

1949 Leaf Jackie Robinson #79

There are those card historians who believe the Leaf cards were issued in late 1948, while others claim they were not released until 1949, which seems more likely. The most important thing to collectors is simply that the set was released. And Robinson is right at home in a set that includes the likes of Joe DiMaggio, Ted Williams, Stan Musial, Honus Wagner and Babe Ruth.

$750–$1,100

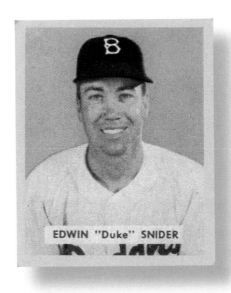

1949 Bowman Duke Snider #226

If anyone should ever ask you what Edwin Snider's Rookie Card looks like . . . well, now you know. Simple card, simple design, high number. And The Duke looks happy to be there, too. For 16 seasons, the Dodgers were happy — no, thrilled — to have him.

$450–$900

1949 BOWMAN ROY CAMPANELLA #84
1949 BOWMAN SATCHEL PAIGE #224

These two cards are grouped together for two reasons: Both men pictured made their major league debuts in 1948 and were pioneers of the game, and both are key Rookie Cards in the '49 Bowman set. Satchel seemed to pitch forever, and was believed to already be in his 40s when he joined the Cleveland Indians. Campy would go on to play a key role in the Brooklyn Dodgers' five NL titles and Brooklyn's only World Series title (1955).

$400–$725 $650–$1,000

1949 BOWMAN EDDIE WAITKUS #142

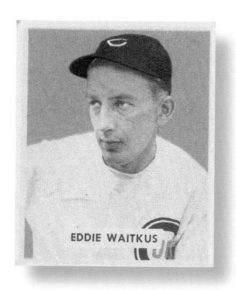

Eddie Waitkus was never called "The Natural." Unlike Roy Hobbs of the fictional New York Knights, Waitkus did not possess heroic power at the plate, nor had he ever literally knocked the cover off the ball. But he was a good first baseman who delivered line drives with a nice left-handed swing. Yet Waitkus *was* Hobbs, before the world had ever heard of Hobbs. Only he was Hobbs off the field, not on it. During the 1949 season, Waitkus — who had been an All-Star with the Cubs in '48 but traded to the Phillies before the '49 season — was shot in a Chicago hotel by a woman he didn't even know, and became the inspiration for Bernard Malamud's "The Natural." Waitkus recovered, returned to the big leagues the next year, and played six more seasons before retiring.

$20–$40

1950

1959

MICKEY MANTLE

The Fabulous Fifties were the golden years for baseball in New York — until the last part of the decade when the Giants departed for San Francisco and the Dodgers left for Los Angeles. But before the lure of California baseball there was New York, where stars such as Willie Mays, Mickey Mantle and Duke Snider shined.

New York teams won eight of the 10 World Series in the decade, and Mantle captured the Triple Crown in 1956, becoming the only switch-hitter to lead the league in average, home runs and RBI. At the time, that helped cement his reputation as the game's greatest slugger.

Joe DiMaggio retired, but was back in the news when he married actress Marilyn Monroe.

EBBETS FIELD

WILLIE MAYS

There was almost as much activity outside the lines as well. Topps emerged as a major competitor to Bowman, and the two companies waged a war for player rights that lasted until 1956 when Topps bought out Bowman. In 1957, the size of the cards themselves shrunk slightly to the 2-1/2 inch by 3-1/2 inch cards we're familiar with today.

Outside of baseball, the world of music was changing quickly. Rock 'n' roll was introduced in America with "Rock Around the Clock," and Elvis Presley released his first hit, "Heartbreak Hotel." Hawaii was inaugurated as our 50th state, cartoonist Charles Schulz introduced his comic strip "Peanuts," and Dr. Seuss published "The Cat in the Hat." Television was a booming business in this country, and it was estimated that, by 1952, most sets were tuned to the weekly antics of Lucille Ball in "I Love Lucy."

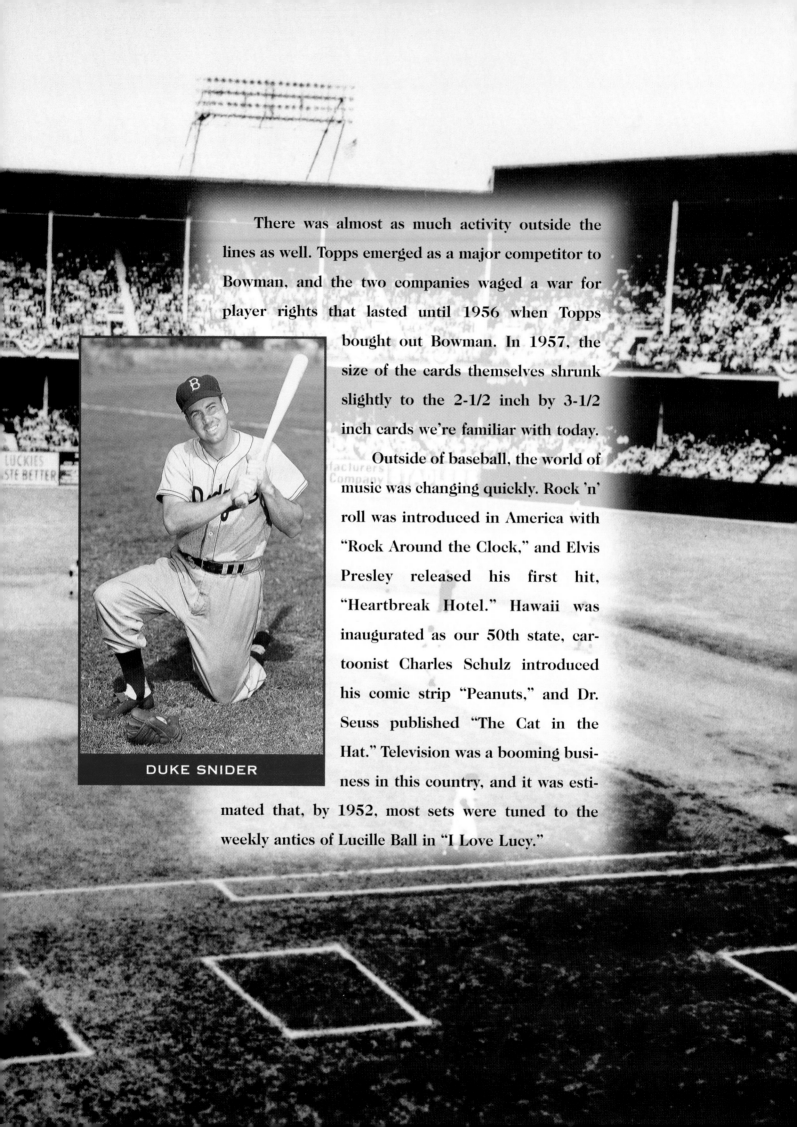

DUKE SNIDER

1950 BOWMAN TED WILLIAMS #98

In 1950, Williams broke out of the gate hot, and he remained so until he fractured his elbow while crashing into the outfield wall making a catch during the All-Star Game. He missed more than 60 games that season, but still collected 97 RBI in 89 games. This card captures Teddy Ballgame at his peak before the troubles began.

$500–$850

1950 BOWMAN JACKIE ROBINSON #22

Brooklyn, Bowman, Baseball . . . it's hard to imagine a more attractive Jackie Robinson card than this low-numbered 1950 issue. It's the second most valuable card in the set, ranking right behind Ted Williams.

$550–$800

1950 BOWMAN YOGI BERRA #46

Yogi's third Bowman card is in the more difficult lower series, as Bowman did not print the card sheets of the various series in equal numbers that year, leaving the first 72 cards in fewer supply. That makes Yogi a bit special. But then, we knew that, right?

Actual question: "Hey Yogi, what time is it?"

Actual answer: "You mean now?"

$200–$325

1951 BOWMAN WHITEY FORD #1

You know what happens when you go 9–1 during your rookie season, then win your only World Series start that same year? You get the honor of leading off the next season's baseball card set, which Whitey did with this Bowman issue.

$500–$800

1951 BOWMAN YOGI BERRA #2

One day, the wife of then New York mayor John Lindsay told Yogi Berra that he looked cool, despite the oppressive heat.

Actual Yogi answer: "You don't look so hot yourself."

On this card, Yogi never looked better.

$175–$275

1951 TOPPS RED BACK YOGI BERRA #1

The first cards Topps issued in pack form were Red Backs, and they featured another card of Yogi in the prime of his career. The '51 Topps cards are commonly known as Red Backs and Blue Backs, because, well, the backs are red or blue. The Red Backs were issued first, and designated as an "A" series while the Blue Backs were a "B" series. Yogi is card #1 in the "A" series, and thus is the leadoff hitter in the long line-up of Topps' cards in packs.

$65–$125

1951 BOWMAN EARLY WYNN #78

It's been said about Early Wynn that he would have thrown at his grandmother if she crowded the plate on him. Here, the 300 game winner and HOFer appears to be lining up for just such a buzz pitch for grandmama.

$30–$55

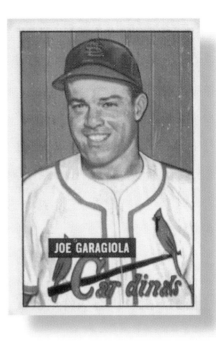

1951 BOWMAN JOE GARAGIOLA #122

Sometimes a player's talent doesn't really emerge until after he retires. Take Charlie Lau, for example, a .255 lifetime hitter before becoming George Brett's batting guru; or Sparky Anderson, who didn't hit a home run and batted just .218 in his only big-league season, but who as a manager led major league clubs to World Championships in both leagues. Then there's Joe Garagiola. Joe was an average ballplayer, but a star personality. Joe looked and acted like everyone's favorite uncle, and that played well during his broadcasting career when he was on the air for NBC's "Baseball Game of the Week" during the 1970s and '80s. He also hosted game shows, hosted the "Today Show" and even did some television commercials for Gerald Ford during the 1976 Presidential campaign. For some guys, all it takes is retirement.

$50–$80

1951 BOWMAN WARREN SPAHN #134

"Spahn and Sain, and pray for rain." In the late 1940s, that was just about the truth for the Boston Braves who were led by Spahn and Johnny Sain. But by the middle of '51, Sain was gone to the Yankees. That left Spahn, who, with his high leg kick,

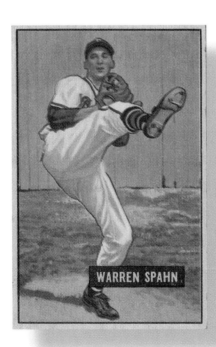

won 22 games and completed an amazing 26 games of the 36 he started.

$75–$125

1951 BOWMAN MICKEY MANTLE #253

This is where it starts for the most important player in baseball card history. No other player has meant more to card collectors than Mickey Mantle, and few Mantle cards — like none, really — are duds. Certainly not this first look at The Mick, before the knee injuries and the Billy and Whitey partying stories set in. You want the real Mantle Rookie Card? This is it, and it's a beauty.

$5,000–$8,500

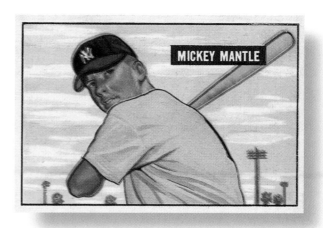

1951 BOWMAN WILLIE MAYS #305

Here's the first card of a player many refer to as the greatest center fielder — or greatest player, period — of all time. When called up to the Giants in '51, Mays struggled to an 0-12 start at the plate, but finally broke out with his first major league hit: a home run off Warren Spahn. He would hit 20 homers as a 20-year-old that season. More importantly for New York fans, Mays added a spark with his everyday play during the '51 campaign. Oh yeah, one more thing; in the words of Russ Hodges:

"The Giants win the pennant!"

"The Giants win the pennant!"

"The Giants win the pennant!"

$2,200–$3,200

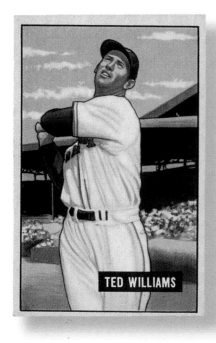

1951 BOWMAN TED WILLIAMS #165

The Bowman Gum Company seemed to be making all the right moves by 1951. Not only had the cardmaker inked Ted Williams to a contract the previous year, but it also increased the size of the baseball cards themselves. More space on the card front meant more space to display the sweet swing of Teddy Ballgame.

$500–$750

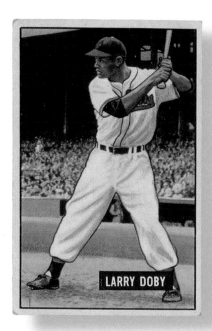

1951 BOWMAN LARRY DOBY #151

The American League's first black ballplayer, Doby was slightly ahead of the Willie, Mickey and the Duke era when he debuted with Cleveland in 1947. His effort to become a good center fielder paid off in 1950 when The Sporting News named him baseball's top center fielder, ahead of such players as Joe DiMaggio and Duke Snider. It was Doby's power that helped set him apart. This card captures Doby's presence like no other: digging in and waiting for his pitch, just before turning on one and sending it 400 feet to the cheap seats.

$35–$65

1952 TOPPS ANDY PAFKO #1

He's the "Rubberband Man" to collectors. Perhaps no card is more misunderstood price-wise than this one. The value of this

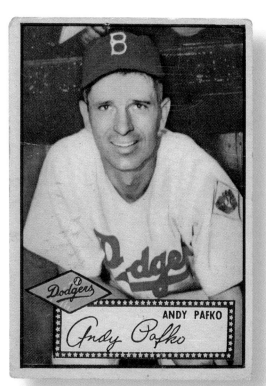

card has to do more with condition than with the ballplayer pictured on it. Pafko was a solid player, and joined Duke Snider and Carl Furillo in the Brooklyn Dodgers' outfield after a trade from the Cubs. But card #1? The designation as card #1 meant that many kids and collectors stuck Handy Andy on the top of the deck, then wrapped the stack with a rubber band. Maybe two rubber bands. Naturally, Pafko's card took more of a beating since it was on top. Now you begin to get the picture. Fewer and fewer high-grade, rubberbandless Pafkos are emerging. And it just so happens that this is from 1952 Topps, the key post-World War II baseball set.

$1,250–$2,500

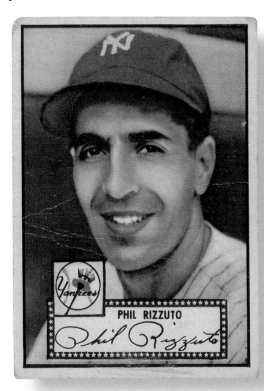

1952 TOPPS PHIL RIZZUTO #11

The Scooter provided a spark to the Yankees during the early part of the 1950s, earning the American League MVP Award in 1950. Kids were pulling out this Rizzuto '52 Topps card smack in the middle of a four-year All-Star run (1950–53) for the Yankee shortstop.

$125–$200

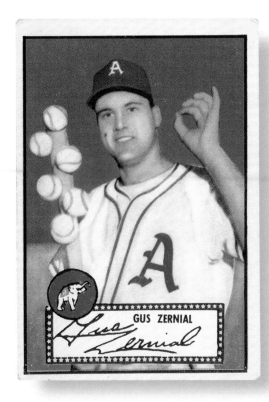

1952 TOPPS GUS ZERNIAL #31

Gus Zernial carried a potent bat, alright. Not only did he lead the AL in home runs in 1951, but during the decade of the '50s, only three AL batters — Mantle being one — hit more homers than Zernial. Yessiree, with a bat in his hands, Gus was A-OK.

$40–$80

1952 TOPPS BOB FELLER #88

Very few superstars can be found in the '52 Topps lower series (1–250). But Bob Feller is there. Rapid Robert from Van Meter, Iowa, was The Rocket of his era. He hurled three no-hitters and 11 one-hitters, and man, could he chuck the ball hard. Somehow, the current generation of baseball fans seems to have glossed over Bob Feller. But for pure heat, Feller could throw with anybody from any generation. We kid you not.

$125–$200

1952 TOPPS BILLY MARTIN #175

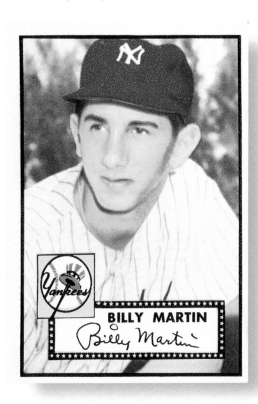

Alfred Manuel Martin was a scrappy kid out of the San Francisco Bay area who arrived at the Yankees clubhouse as yet another prospect from the West Coast. It didn't take long for Billy to write the book on himself: clutch player, lots of fights on and off the field, winner. This card captures Billy long before his managerial days with the Yankees, before the bickering with George Steinbrenner, Reggie Jackson or whatever marshmallow salesman happened to challenge Billy that day. For the Billy on this card, the future lay far ahead.

$200–$300

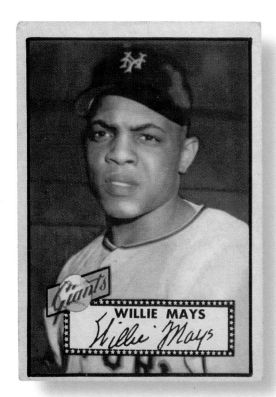

1952 TOPPS WILLIE MAYS #261

As Topps' first card of Mays, this release carries a great deal of historical significance. This card often is referred to as Mays' Rookie Card, but it's not. It is a great card, though, and would be the centerpiece in many collections. Even better is the fact that it doesn't fall in the high-number series. For the price of some of the high-number cards, a collector could instead buy a '52 Mays in decent condition. And that's not a bad deal at all.

$1,500–$2,500

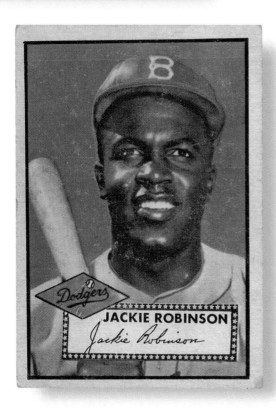

1952 TOPPS MICKEY MANTLE #311

What a great card this is. Easily the most sought after post-war card, and the poster child for the modern baseball card hobby. It's the second Mantle card issued, but the first Topps Mantle card. It's position as the first card in the legendary '52 Topps high-number series only adds to its already skyrocketing appeal. You want history? You want nostalgia? You want the card hobby all rolled into one piece of cardboard? You've got it with the '52 Topps Mantle.

$1,200–$1,800

1952 TOPPS JACKIE ROBINSON #312

Jackie Robinson worked out a deal with Topps in time to be included in the high-number series of 1952. Having Jackie in the set was quite a boon for Topps, as the Dodger second baseman was a legitimate star and collector favorite.

$900–$1,500

1952 BOWMAN WILLIE MAYS #218

The second Bowman issue of the No. 3 man on baseball's all-time home run list. Willie is part of the '52 Bowman high-number series, and his card is the second most valuable issue in the set behind Mickey Mantle.

$800–$1,200

1952 BOWMAN MICKEY MANTLE #101

At the start of the 1952 season, Mickey Mantle had done a lot of growing up, maybe more than a 20-year-old should be expected to do at one time. It started in the fall of '51, when he tore ligaments in his right knee during his first World Series game. That was followed by pressure from off-season rumors of replacing the retired Joe DiMaggio in center field and the death of Mick's father at age 39. So, back in '52, being Mickey Mantle wasn't all it was cracked up to be. This '52 Bowman card seems to capture the mood at the time.

$1,500–$2,500

1952 BOWMAN DUKE SNIDER #116

While New York had Mantle and Mays, Brooklyn had The Duke. In '52 he made the locals proud, finishing at .303-21-92 at the plate and a sterling .992 in the field. When fans asked, "Who's the best center fielder in New York?" Brooklynites believed they had the answer.

$120–$200

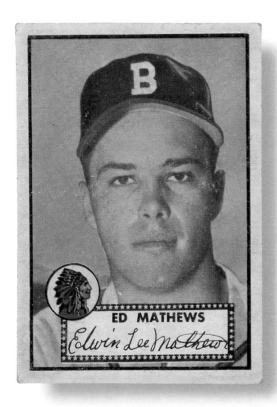

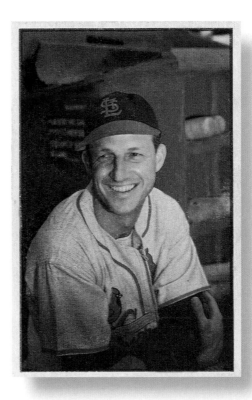

1952 TOPPS EDDIE MATHEWS #407

The final card in any old set is legendary for the amount of damage it receives from being at the bottom of the stack. The last card in a set also can be difficult to obtain, simply because fewer of the cards were produced in the later series. That's the story with this Eddie Mathews Rookie Card. Eddie was a fantastic prospect for the Braves in '52. It just so happens that his RC is (a) in the classic '52 Topps set; and (b) the final card in the set, and thus a high number. That all translates to instant baseball card greatness.

$3,000–$4,500

1953 BOWMAN COLOR STAN MUSIAL #32

While this is a nice shot of The Man, the real importance of this card lies in the fact that, after it was released, Musial did not appear on another major card manufacturer's issue for five years. A lot can happen in five years. Teams can move from one side of the country to the other (see "Giants" and "Dodgers"), a guy can make it big with a song called "Hound Dog," and Stan Musial can disappear from mainstream sets.

$350–$700

1953 BOWMAN COLOR PEE WEE REESE #33

When art meets sport, you get something really beautiful.

$500–$1,000

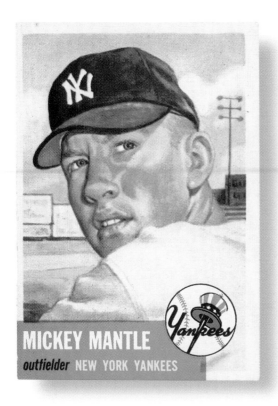

1953 TOPPS MICKEY MANTLE #82

Many advanced collectors consider this to be the most attractive Mantle card issued during the first five years of his career. This card became especially popular in '53 when word circulated of his 565-foot home run off Chuck Stobbs. Speed, power and charisma all in one package.

$2,000–$3,000

1953 BOWMAN COLOR MICKEY MANTLE #59

Is this a baseball card, or what? Sunny day, blue sky, Yankee Stadium and Mickey Mantle. Perfect.

$1,800–$3,000

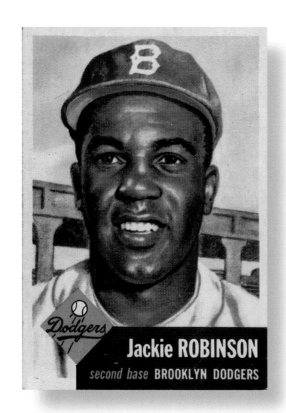

1953 TOPPS JACKIE ROBINSON #1

Jackie graced the first card of the '53 Topps series and helped set a trend that saw Ted Williams, Willie Mays and Hank Aaron follow as the first card in later sets. And just in case you — or collectors of that era — forgot who Robinson played for, yes, that is the Brooklyn Bridge painted behind him.

$250–$500

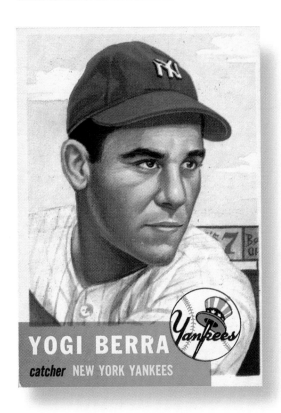

YOGI BERRA
catcher NEW YORK YANKEES

1953 TOPPS YOGI BERRA #104

Yogi's '53 Topps card falls right between the double-printed Joe Astroth and the double-printed Joe Nuxhall. But Berra is not a double print. Perhaps Topps knew the world wasn't ready for a double dosing of Yogi.

$125–$225

1953 BOWMAN COLOR YOGI BERRA, HANK BAUER, MICKEY MANTLE #44

One of the first multi-player cards in the hobby, and a good one at that. Bauer was a roommate of Mantle's during The Mick's early years in New York. Looks like Hank is amused at something in the shot, while Mickey is studiously checking out the play on the field. But just what in the world is Yogi doing?

$475–$675

WILLIE MAYS
outfielder NEW YORK GIANTS

1953 TOPPS WILLIE MAYS #244

Willie Mays spent the entire 1953 season in military service, yet Topps still produced a card of him. And just to make it interesting while Willie was away, Topps stuck it in the tough high-number series. Say Hey.

$1,800–$2,700

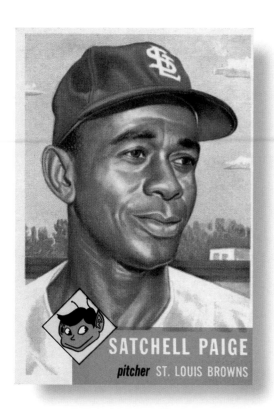

1954 BOWMAN MICKEY MANTLE #65

It seems Bowman took a different approach with its 1954 set, going from art-like 1953 color photographs to the more "colorized photo" look of the '54 cards. Even so, this isn't a bad likeness of The Mick.

$900–$1,400

1953 TOPPS SATCHEL PAIGE #220

While it's admirable that Topps included Paige in the '53 set (right before the high-number series), the company should have checked the spelling of his first name. "Satchell" is incorrect. It was never corrected, but what the heck. There's 'ol Satch, in a St. Louis Browns jersey no less. Paige would have been close to 47 years old at the time this card was released, but he was coming off a 12–10 season in which his ERA was an impressive 3.07. Obviously he could still pitch, and pitch effectively. Topps thought so, too. This is the only Topps Satchel Paige card, and one of just a few major issues the HOFer appeared on.

$250–$450

1954 WILSON WEINERS ROY CAMPANELLA

Don't be fooled; it only looks as if Campy is thinking about lunch.

$375–$750

1954 BOWMAN NELSON FOX #6

Proper technique at second base, brought to you by Nelson Fox. Do you think Nellie *knows* the ball is already in his glove?

$45–$75

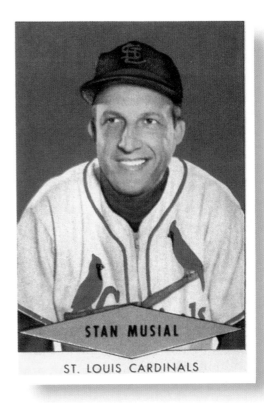

1954 RED HEART STAN MUSIAL

Take a look at one of the only Stan Musial cards issued in 1954. It wasn't available in gum packs, potato chips or any other confectionery or salty snack product. Instead, it took two can labels of Red Heart Dog Food and a dime to order a series of these beauties. Stan The Man is a short print, as are all the cards with red backgrounds in the 33-card set.

$200–$400

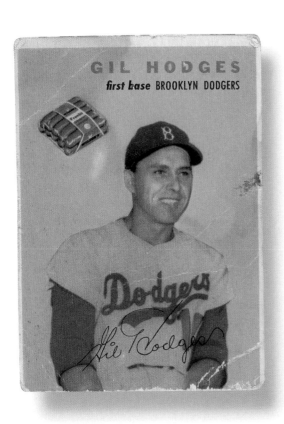

1954 WILSON WEINERS GIL HODGES

If we didn't know better, we'd say the unsuspecting Mr. Hodges is about to be bopped with a package of winged weinies. But we know better. The "floating" franks added to the appeal of the Wilson set, a set in which collectors received one card — often one greasy card — in packages of hot dogs. Gil is among the most valuable cards in the unnumbered 20-card set, ranking only behind HOFers Ted Williams, Roy Campanella and Bob Feller.

$200–$400

1954 BOWMAN TED WILLIAMS #66A

In 1954, there was a war being waged in the candy aisle between Bowman and Topps. Each had a heavy hitter on its side: Mickey Mantle for Bowman, Ted Williams for Topps. So it was quite a shock to the folks at Topps when Ted Williams — their guy — was on a Bowman card, right there next to Mantle. Hey, it was a bit of a shock to Williams as well. Whether it was Williams or Topps or both who took action, the fact is the Williams Bowman card was pulled from production and distribution early and replaced by another fine Red Sox outfielder, Jimmy Piersall. Bottom line: This is one tough Ted to find.

$2,700–$4,500

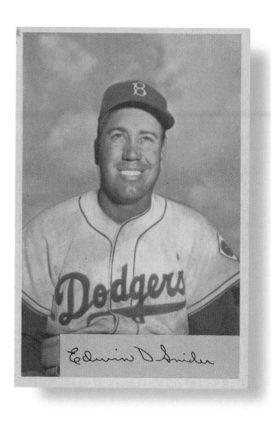

1954 BOWMAN DUKE SNIDER #170

He is The Duke of Flatbush.

$75–$135

1954 BOWMAN WILLIE MAYS #89

Check out the facsimile autograph on this card. Either Willie forgot the "s" on his name, or the signature was picked up off a contract or other document without the "s." Problem is, you can't really have Willie Mays without the "s." Even so, this is a great card from a great year for Mays. How great? The NL Most Valuable Player Award, a league-leading .345 average, 41 home runs and the catch of a lifetime in the 1954 World Series.

$250–$400

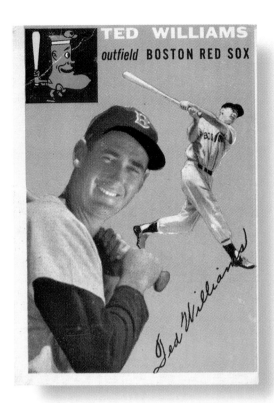

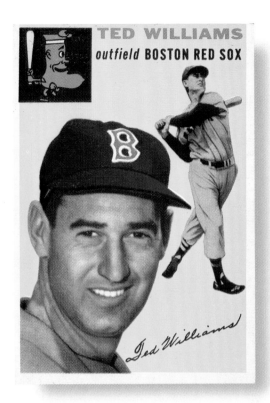

1954 TOPPS TED WILLIAMS #1　　　　**1954 TOPPS TED WILLIAMS #250**

Talk about classic bookends . . . Perhaps wanting to get mileage out of its exclusive relationship with Williams, Topps gave The Splendid Splinter not one, but two cards. He opened the set, then closed it. With Mantle under contract with Bowman and Musial not in either Bowman or Topps sets, Topps played its best player twice. The cardmaker would do the same thing 21 years later when Hank Aaron opened and closed the 1975 Topps set.

$400–$700　　　　　　　　　　　　　*$500–$800*

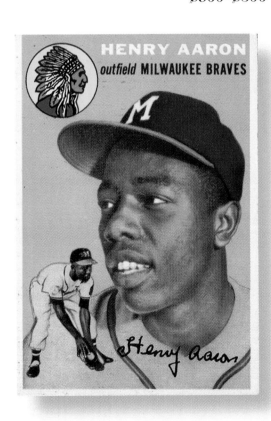

1954 TOPPS HANK AARON #128

The 1954 Topps set holds a lot of Rookie Cards, but none more important — none even close — than this one of Major League Baseball's all-time home run king. We can think of 755 reasons why we like this card.

$1,000–$1,500

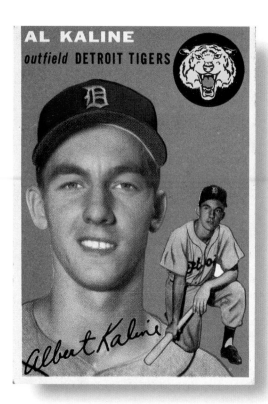

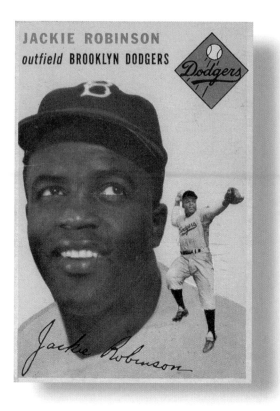

1954 TOPPS AL KALINE #201

If only the Philadelphia Athletics had coughed up a little money, Hall of Famer Al Kaline might have been spreading out his 3,007 career hits in the City of Brotherly Love. But, alas, the frugal A's would have nothing to do with a signing bonus. *"We would like to have the Kalina* (sic) *boy,"* A's general manager Arthur Ehlers wrote to scout John Brennan in a letter dated May 18, 1953. *"However, I don't want him as a bonus player. You can sign him to an Ottawa contract, however he must not make more than Four Thousand Dollars including salary and bonus."* The Detroit Tigers had no problem signing Kaline to a bonus, and just two years after Ehlers' note, Kaline led the American League in batting (.343) at the tender age of 20.

$500–$750

1954 TOPPS JACKIE ROBINSON #10

Jackie was just beginning the downward slope of his career, but he could still run with the best of them. He could still turn on the jet boosters when he needed to. The lower number designated for this card makes it one of the more accessible Topps Jackie Robinson cards to collectors wanting to add a legend to their collections.

$200–$300

1954 TOPPS O'BRIEN BROTHERS #139

What great athletes these twins were. That's Eddie on the left, and Johnny on the right. Or is it Johnny on the left, and Eddie on the right? Whatever, the O'Briens are on the card together which indicates Topps was trying to mix some innovation into the normal card routine. At one time this card was rumored to be short-printed, but that doesn't appear to be the case. Still, this remains a popular card with collectors who — like the O'Briens — appreciate getting two for one.

$20–$40

1954 TOPPS TOMMY LASORDA #132

In parts of three major league seasons, Lasorda was 0–4 with a 6.48 ERA. In one outing, he tied a major league record with three wild pitches in one inning. So perhaps it's not surprising that this is Tommy's only big-league card as an active player. But thank God for life after a playing career. Indeed, if it hadn't been for Tommy's rather unspectacular major league career, the world might never have heard of any human being anywhere bleeding Dodger blue.

$100–$200

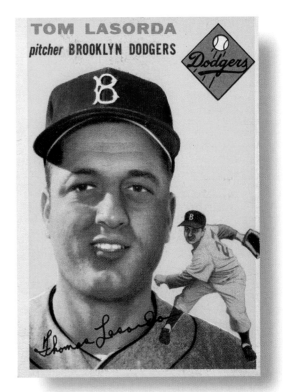

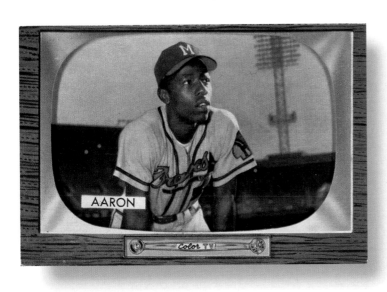

1955 BOWMAN HANK AARON #179

Like any good television program that's run its course, the Bowman line of baseball cards came to an end after the ambitious 1955 TV release. It wasn't bad ratings that brought Bowman down; it was rival Topps, which had purchased its competitor and sat dormant on the name before resurrecting it again in 1989. But Bowman did the right thing in getting that young Milwaukee Braves outfielder in the set — the same player the company missed including in 1954. But The Hammer is there in '55. If you want a Bowman Hank Aaron card, here's your one and only choice.

$125–$200

1954 TOPPS ERNIE BANKS #94

With all due respect to Gabby Hartnett, Billy Williams, Ryne Sandberg, Andre Dawson and Sammy Sosa and his 66, Ernie Banks is the most popular Cubbie ever to take his cuts in Wrigley.

Banks won back-to-back MVP awards (1958–59), whacked 512 career home runs, was named to 11 All-Star teams and kept his smile even in the down years — and there were plenty of those during Banks' tenure on the North Side. Clearly, this Rookie Card will cost a collector a bit more than a couple bleacher seats this side of Waveland or Sheffield Avenues.

$500–$750

1955 BOWMAN MICKEY MANTLE #202

As mistakes go, the error on the back of the '55 Bowman Mantle card is pretty mild. The card, an uncorrected error, lists Mickey's birthday as Oct. 30, 1931, instead of the correct date of Oct. 20, 1931. In other words, Bowman tried to make Mantle 10 days younger than he actually was. There was a time during the latter part of his career when The Mick would have been thrilled to at least *feel* 10 days younger, if nothing else.

$600–$900

1955 TOPPS HANK AARON #47

An attractive and more affordable alternative to the '54 Topps Aaron RC is this second-year Topps card, conveniently placed in a lower series and thus not a part of any high-number hype. While Hank displays his swing on the secondary photo in this card, there's still no hint that he would someday become the greatest home run hitter in major league history.

$200–$350

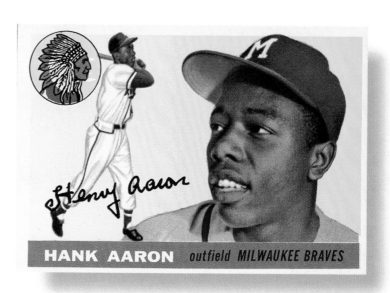

1955 BOWMAN JOCKO CONLAN #303

Don't you know that with a name like Jocko, you've got to be able to take care of yourself. And that wasn't a problem for Conlan. He got his start as an umpire while still an active major league player, which certainly provided him a rare perspective to the game. Bowman thought umpires were cool enough to include in its '55 set, and Jocko — elected to the Hall of Fame in 1974 — is a highlight of that arbitrator subset. Conlan was loud, but fair. His battles with managers Leo "The Lip" Durocher and Frankie Frisch are legendary. Rest assured, Jocko got the last word.

$50–$75

1955 TOPPS ROBERTO CLEMENTE #164

What in the world were the Dodgers thinking? They had a brilliant young prospect in their organization, and they chose to play games. It ended up costing them $6,000 and Roberto Clemente. Here's the deal: Brooklyn signed Clemente out of high school, giving him a $10,000 bonus. In 1954, his first season in the organization, he played for Montreal, then one of the Dodgers' minor league affiliates. But a rule in place in professional baseball at the time called for any player signed for more than $4,000 to be placed on the major league roster after one year of minor league service. If the player was not added to the roster, any other club could sign that player for $4,000. The Dodgers opted not to add Clemente to the roster, and instead tried to "hide" him in Montreal by not playing him. Bad move. Pirates scout Clyde Sukeforth saw Clemente and recognized pure talent. The Pirates claimed him during the off-season for $4,000, making him one of the greatest bargains in major league history. Give Topps' scouts credit, too, for including a player that had never played in the majors in its '55 set.

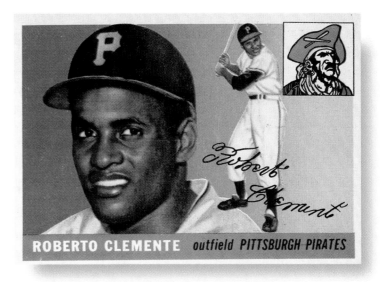

ROBERTO CLEMENTE *outfield* PITTSBURGH PIRATES

$1,500–$2,200

1955 TOPPS HARRY AGGANIS #152

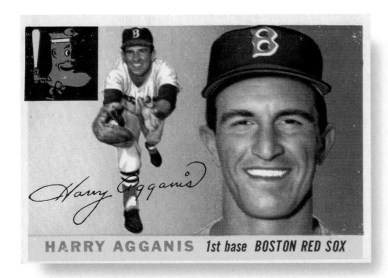

HARRY AGGANIS *1st base* BOSTON RED SOX

The Golden Greek was considered to be one of the greatest athletes the Boston area ever produced. A college football quarterback legend at Boston University, Agganis was a first-round pick of the Cleveland Browns, who offered him a $25,000 bonus to sign. But up stepped the Boston Red Sox with an even higher signing bonus, and Agganis turned to baseball as a left-handed, power-hitting first baseman. In the early part of 1955, he was batting over .300 and appeared to be a star in the making when he was suddenly hospitalized with pneumonia. After his release, he returned to the Red Sox lineup but fell ill again in June and was again hospitalized. He never made it back to baseball, dying suddenly at age 26 of a massive pulmonary embolism on June 27, 1955. This '55 Agganis card is in Topps' "semi-high" series, and was released shortly before Agganis' illness was yet known.

$40–$70

1955 TOPPS HARMON KILLEBREW #124

If not for injuries that wiped out parts of two seasons, Harmon Killebrew — the hands-down best player ever to come out of Payette, Idaho — would certainly have reached 600 home runs. Still, his 573 round-trippers are second most by an American Leaguer, behind only Babe Ruth for AL sluggers. And while other players may eventually pass Killebrew in the record books, nobody can ever take away the

530-foot shot to left in old Metropolitan Stadium that splintered two seats. Nor can anyone ever take away the blast that completely cleared the left field roof in Tiger Stadium, which just three other players (Frank Howard, Cecil Fielder, Mark McGwire) have ever done in the 87-year history of the venerable stadium. Power was the name of the game, and The Killer had plenty of it. And such nice handwriting, too.

$150–$250

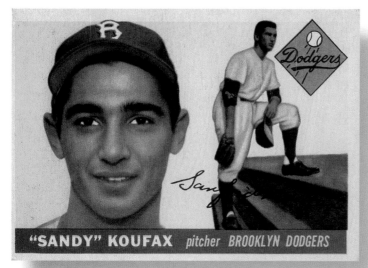

1955 TOPPS SANDY KOUFAX #123

At the time of this card's release, Sanford Koufax was just 19 years old and pitching for his hometown Brooklyn Dodgers. Great work for a kid, if you can get it.

$550–$900

1956 TOPPS MICKEY MANTLE #135

The 1956 season was Mantle's favorite, and his '56 Topps card is a favorite among collectors. For one thing, it came during the first of three MVP seasons. For another, that's one sweet catch The Mick is stretching out to make at the wall in right field.

$900–$1,400

1956 TOPPS ROBERTO CLEMENTE #33

The second Clemente card may even be more attractive than the first, and that's saying something. But having a real game action shot in the background of the card front added a great deal to the '56 cards. Topps was still referring to Clemente as Roberto in '56. By the next year, the company "Americanized" Clemente by calling him "Bob" on his card.

$225–$375

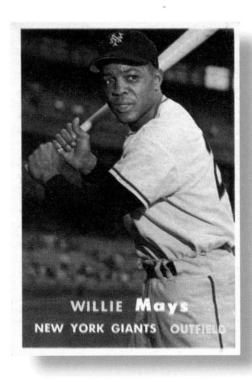

1956 TOPPS HANK AARON #31

Call this two superstars for the price of one. While that definitely is Henry Aaron in the big photo (the same picture used on his '54 and '55 Topps cards, by the way), that's not Aaron sliding into home. That's actually another pretty fair ballplayer, Willie Mays. Yes, that's a Milwaukee uniform the sliding player has on but it was painted on by the artist. That photo of Mays sliding actually appeared in a baseball publication a year before appearing on Hank Aaron's baseball card.

$150–$275

1957 TOPPS WILLIE MAYS #10

This is how many New Yorkers remember Mays: confident, bat in hand and Polo Grounds over his shoulder. In '57, the Giants' final season in the Big Apple, Mays not only legged out 20 triples, but he also chased down a lot of fly balls in center field, earning the first of 12 consecutive Gold Glove awards.

$125–$225

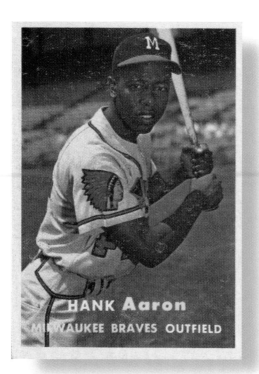

1957 TOPPS HANK AARON #20

What's this, Henry Aaron being a joker? Not at all. Hank never batted left-handed. Instead, Topps simply reversed the negative, which is obvious by looking at the "44" on the front of Aaron's uniform.

$125–$200

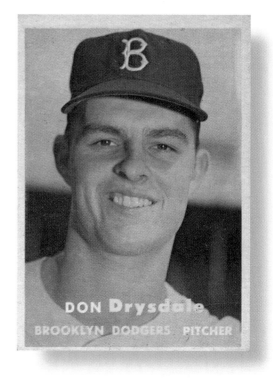

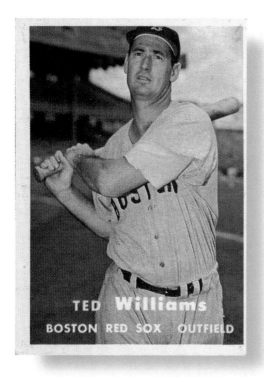

1957 TOPPS TED WILLIAMS #1

Understand this: At age 39, most of us are happy to leg out a single in softball without pulling anything really important in our bodies. At 39, the only thing Ted Williams was pulling was pitches down the right field line. A lot of pitches were smacked for a lot of hits. Midway through the season it was obvious that Teddy Ballgame was onto something wonderful. Sixteen years after hitting .406, Williams was again flirting with .400. He fell short, but not by much, finishing at an incredible .388 with 38 home runs. At 39, Williams was still very much The Kid.

$250–$500

1957 TOPPS DON DRYSDALE #18

Don Drysdale threw hard, and while paired with Sandy Koufax during the late 1950s and part of the '60s, afforded the Dodgers baseball's best 1–2 punch. Drysdale logged six seasons of 200 or more strikeouts, and his best season came in 1962 when he went 25-9 with a 2.83 ERA. "Big D" worked the corners of the plate and wasn't afraid to dust off a hitter if he got too close. But did you know that Drysdale led the NL in hit batsmen five times, and set a modern record by hitting 154 batters in his career? Ouch.

$125–$225

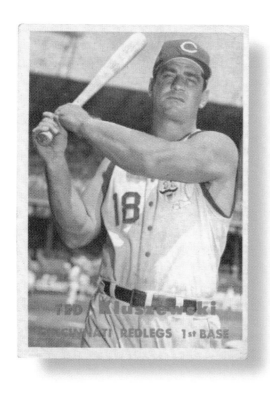

1957 TOPPS TED KLUSZEWSKI #165

What was a collector to do in 1957? There was Ted Kazanski, and there was Ted Kluszewski. It could get down-right confusing. Ted Kazanski was the light-hitting second baseman for the Philadelphia Phillies who had slugged 11 career home runs entering the '57 season; Ted Kluszewski was the slugging first baseman for the Cincinnati Reds who led the NL in home runs in 1954, and who had slugged 40 or more homers in three of the previous four seasons. Ted Kazanski's uniform included sleeves, but Ted Kluszewski's uniform was sleeveless in order to accommodate his growing biceps. So you can understand how a collector could have mixed up the two in '57, right?

$35–$60

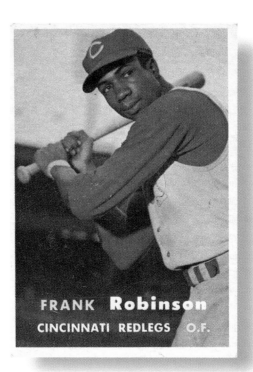

1957 TOPPS FRANK ROBINSON #35

The 1956 season was a coming out party for Frank Robinson, whose 38 home runs established a then major-league record for most homers hit by a rookie (since broken by Mark McGwire with 49 in 1987). Reds fans must have been anticipating the first card appearance of their newest star, and the classy look of the Robby RC delivered.

$130–$200

1957 TOPPS MICKEY MANTLE #95

Two versions of this card exist: one with man in background and one without man. Topps chose to airbrush out the man in the background of the Mantle photo used on the front of The Mick's '57 card so that Mickey wasn't competing for collectors' attention (as if that ever would have happened). But even after the airbrush, the man could still faintly be seen. So Topps tried it again with better results. Both versions can be found on the secondary market.

$700–$1,000

1957 Topps Power Hitters (Mantle/Berra) #407

Topps introduced star combination cards in 1957 to rave reviews. But then, who wouldn't love a classic taken-on-the-steps-of-the-dugout shot of Mickey Mantle and Yogi Berra? This is the final card in the '57 set.

$350–$500

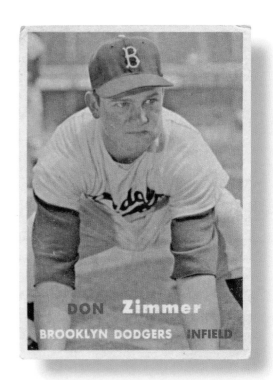

1957 Topps Brooks Robinson #328

The Human Vacuum Cleaner's first card appears in the tough '57 semi-high number series, making it the most valuable of the 1957 Topps Rookie Cards. In 16 of his 23 seasons at the hot corner, Brooksie was gold, winning Gold Gloves every year from 1960–75. He still holds most all of baseball's fielding records for a third baseman and will likely be the sole holder of those marks for quite some time.

$250–$400

1957 Topps Don Zimmer #284

Don Zimmer is what baseball is all about. Tough, scrappy and full of strategy. Zim, now a successful coach and manager, was the second baseman for the 1955 world champion Brooklyn Dodgers, but hardly anyone remembers that. Instead, they remember that he has a metal plate in his head, inserted after he was struck in the noggin with a pitch in 1953. In 1956, he was struck in the face with a pitch while with Brooklyn. All of which may help explain the look on Popeye's face.

$20–$35

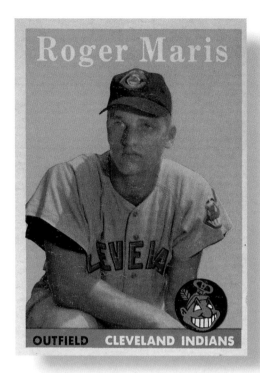

1958 TOPPS ROGER MARIS #47

It couldn't have been easy being Roger Maris. Raised in North Dakota, far from the skyscrapers of New York City, Maris was perhaps unprepared for what the next 10 years would do to his life at the time of this card's release. For starters, there was a trade to the Yankees from the Indians. Then there were the 61 homers in 1961, and finally another trade, this one to the pennant-winning St. Louis Cardinals. Cards from '58 Topps Series I are difficult to find in good condition, so a clean copy of this card is a double bonus.

$275–$450

1958 TOPPS STAN MUSIAL ALL-STAR #476

After 16 full seasons in the major leagues, Stan Musial finally got around to signing that Topps contract that allows for usage of a player's likeness on baseball cards. This is the first Topps Musial card, and, apparently, Topps was so thrilled to have The Man aboard that they triple-printed it.

$20–$40

1958 TOPPS WORLD SERIES BATTING FOES #418

Take your pick; we like our chances with either of these guys.

$175–$275

1958 TOPPS MICKEY MANTLE ALL-STAR #487

Another triple print in Topps' high-number All-Star subset in '58. This is the same card NBC sportscaster Bob Costas has carried in his wallet for years. Bob's is no longer Mint, by the way.

$100–$175

1959 TOPPS GEORGE ANDERSON #338

George Anderson spent one season in the big leagues, but he didn't hit a home run in the 477 at-bats he logged in 1959. Oh, he came close. "I took [Don] Drysdale deep," Anderson once told a throng of reporters. When eyebrows raised in amazement, Anderson delivered the kicker: " . . . just foul." But as Sparky Anderson, he forged a Hall of Fame career that saw him win more than 2,000 games and capture World Series titles with the Cincinnati Reds and Detroit Tigers. And that's no joke.

$30–$60

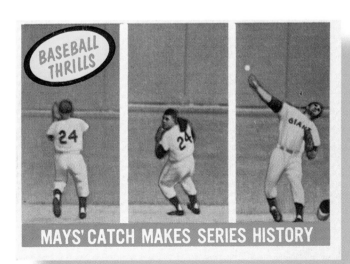

1959 TOPPS "MAYS' CATCH MAKES SERIES HISTORY" #464

Long before instant replay, VCRs and the rewind button, there were simple photographs. Topps used the simple photograph to perfection in replaying Willie Mays' spectacular catch in the 1954 World Series. The sequence also catches one of the most underrated aspects of the entire play, Mays spinning around in one motion and making a dead-on throw to second baseman Davey Williams that prevented two base runners from scoring.

$25–$40

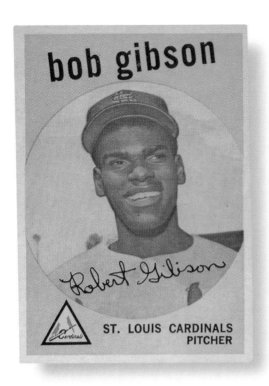

1959 TOPPS BOB GIBSON #514

Look at Bob's face; you'd smile too if you threw a wicked fastball, had pinpoint control and were afraid of nothing. *Nothing.* That was the greatness of Bob Gibson. Be warned: This is a difficult high-number card to find perfectly centered.

$125–$250

Jan. 23, 1959 — Ted Signs For 1959

1959 FLEER TED WILLIAMS "TED SIGNS FOR 1959" #68

You've got to hand it to Fleer. Even 40 years ago they knew how to play the game. Back in 1959, when the company faced the prospect of competing against Topps, Fleer's execs did something remarkable: They signed Ted Williams away from Topps. Then they created an entire set around The Splendid Splinter. That was fine until Topps got word of card #68 in Fleer's Ted Williams set, which pictures Ted about to sign a contract with Red Sox GM Bucky Harris — the same Bucky Harris who happened to be Topps' property at the time. Well, you can imagine Topps' feelings on the matter. Rather than face a lawsuit, Fleer withdrew card #68 by defacing the lower right corner of the card on the printing sheet, and then destroying those cards after they were cut from the sheet. An undetermined number of Mint #68 cards did make it into packs before Fleer took action, but it didn't take long for collectors building a set to pinpoint the real toughie of the bunch — card #68.

$500–$1,000

1959 TOPPS ROY CAMPANELLA "SYMBOL OF COURAGE" #550

What a hero and beloved man Roy Campanella was. Even though he never played a game in Los Angeles, more than 93,000 fans attended a tribute for him at the Coliseum in May 1959. Campy's courageous battle to remain active, after a terrible automobile accident paralyzed him from the waist down in 1958, is documented on this card. And the text on the back is credited to Warren Giles, then the NL president. Topps' decision to honor Campanella — a three-time NL MVP — was classy. Kind of like Campy himself.

$100–$160

Fleer, which had entered the baseball card field in 1959 with the Ted Williams set, tried to go head-to-head with giant Topps during the early 1960s, releasing old-timer sets in 1960 and '61. But outside of Williams (then still Fleer property) in 1960, none of the sets featured active players, which put Fleer at a considerable disadvantage.

In 1963, Fleer tried to even the playing field by releasing its own 66-card set featuring current players. But to avoid conflict with Topps, Fleer packaged a cookie with its cards instead of bubble gum. It didn't work. Topps took Fleer to court and won, effectively removing Fleer from the baseball card market (the company did produce some cartoon-like World Series cards) for the next 18 years.

Topps would rule the remainder of the decade, and the final set of the '60s — 1969 — also featured the final regular issue card of Mickey Mantle, which included his complete career statistics.

The exploits of Mantle and the Yankees helped soothe the nation's troubled soul during the decade. John F. Kennedy was inaugurated as the 35th President of the United States in 1961, the same year Roger Maris eclipsed Babe Ruth as the single-season home run champion. Two years later, the country

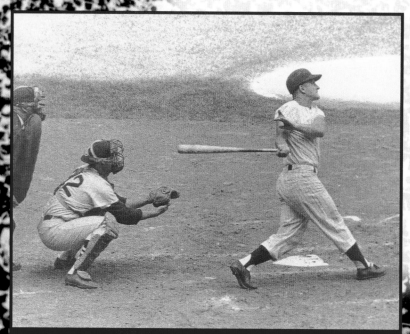

ROGER MARIS

mourned the asassination of JFK. The decade also saw the assassinations of civil rights leader Dr. Martin Luther King Jr. and Robert F. Kennedy. The United States became heavily involved in the Vietnam War, setting off anti-war demonstrations from coast to coast including one at the 1968 Democratic National Convention in Chicago in which demonstrators were beaten by police.

BOB GIBSON

Other troubles ensued: Marilyn Monroe died of an apparent suicide, although questions surrounding the death remain today, and civil unrest prevailed in many cities including Detroit and the Watts section of Los Angeles.

But there were plenty of good things happening in the '60s: Motown Records was created by Berry Gordy, the Beatles hit America running and were a huge sensation, Wilt Chamberlain scored 100 points in a game, the Houston Astrodome opened as the first covered stadium and Neil Armstrong was the first man to step on the moon, representing "one small step for man, and one giant leap for mankind."

SHEA STADIUM

1960 TOPPS MICKEY MANTLE #563

By 1960, it wasn't a matter of *if* Mantle would be an All-Star, it was whether he would bat third, fourth or fifth. He was a guaranteed show no matter how he was playing during the season. This card represents a sort of transition, as the '50s were over and the '60s were just starting. And Mickey still had plenty of Mantlesque thrills ahead of him including another MVP Award and another 50-plus home run season.

$225–$325

1960 TOPPS CARL YASTRZEMSKI #148

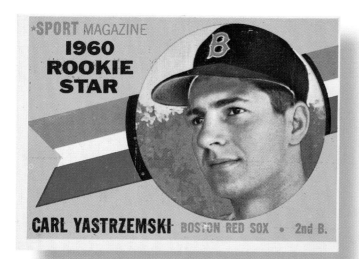

The new kid in Beantown had a funny name and an even funnier bat-high stance at the plate, but Yaz had the last laugh by seamlessly replacing Ted Williams in Boston's left field after Ted's retirement. In 23 seasons, Yaz collected three batting titles, 3,419 hits and six Gold Gloves. He led the Red Sox to the World Series in 1967, the same year he won the Triple Crown — the last player in the major leagues to capture a Triple Crown. As for this Rookie Card, print marks on some copies make this a great find in truly Mint condition.

$80–$140

1960 TOPPS WILLIE McCOVEY #316

As far as debuts go, Willie "Stretch" McCovey's in 1959 might not have been the best ever, but it was big: a 4-for-4 day with two triples off Hall of Famer Robin Roberts. McCovey went on to win the NL Rookie of the Year Award in '59, and was no secret to collectors getting their first glimpse of his card in 1960. Ten years after his ROY season, Mac won the National League MVP Award with the Giants. His awesome power led to three home run titles, and his shots were always the high, majestic kind — there was nothing cheap about a McCovey home

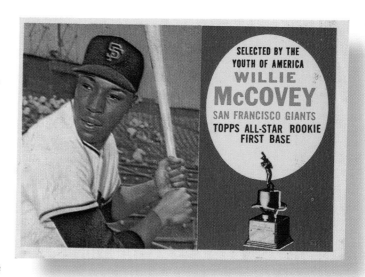

run. For a guy who opened his career with a bang, he closed it with 512 home runs and induction into the Hall of Fame. During the decade of the '60s, McCovey might have been the game's most feared and dominant home run hitter. And that's no Stretch.

$70–$115

1960 FLEER TED WILLIAMS #72

The Pepper Martin card-back short print from this set may get more publicity, but this is the last regular-issue card released while Teddy Ballgame was still an active player. Williams, in fact, was the only active player included in the 79-card set as Fleer still held his card rights. At age 42, Williams hit .316 with 29 home runs and 72 RBI before retiring after the season. His 75 walks in 1960 were nearly double the amount of strikeouts. With typical Williams flair, The Splendid Splinter belted a home run in his final at-bat (the 521st round-tripper of his career), leaving the Fenway Park crowd cheering. Within weeks of that moment, he was out on the lake, doing what he really wanted to do in life: fish.

$45–$90

1961 TOPPS ROGER MARIS #2

While Maris and Mickey Mantle chased the legend of Babe Ruth in the summer of '61, baseball card collectors chased this card out of Series 1 packs. By the final game of the season, when Maris sent Tracy Stallard's pitch over the right field fence for home run #61, this was the card everyone wanted to trade for.

$100–$175

1961 TOPPS BILLY WILLIAMS #141

You would think a young player who comes into the league and hits 25 homers and collects 86 RBI as a rookie would get plenty of attention. In these days of hyped Rookie Cards he certainly would. But not in 1961. Not when Mickey Mantle and Roger Maris were grabbing the headlines. This is a nice card of a Hall of Fame player. But it's obvious that sometimes in life, timing is everything.

$30–$60

1961 TOPPS "LARSEN PITCHES PERFECT GAME" #402

Don Larsen was a sub-.500 pitcher with seven different teams in his career, but for one day he was perfect. On Oct. 8, 1956, 27 Brooklyn Dodgers stepped in against Larsen and 27 Dodgers went down against Larsen. Pitching for the Yankees that day, Don was unhittable. It still stands as the only perfect game in World Series history. That's Billy Martin just behind Larsen, ready for anything coming his way.

$15–$30

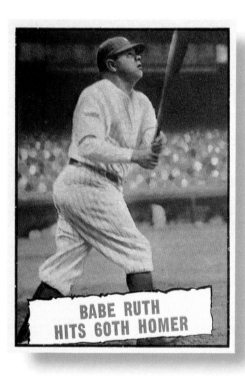

1961 TOPPS "BABE RUTH HITS 60TH HOMER" #401

So let's get this straight; In 1961, Topps decides to issue a card honoring Babe Ruth's 60th home run as part of its "Baseball Thrills" subset. After all, who would ever break that record? The card is issued just months before Roger Maris passes The Babe with home run No. 61. What are the odds?!?!

$30–$50

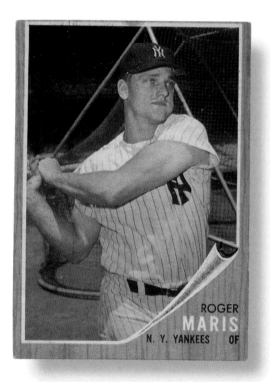

1962 TOPPS ROGER MARIS #1

It should come as a surprise to no one that Topps chose Maris to kick off its 1962 set. Roger, coming off back-to-back MVP seasons and the 61 home runs in '61, would record his last 100-RBI season as a major leaguer in 1962. The fact that this card is a #1 and includes the 61 home runs on the card back makes it a worthy and desirable addition.

$125–$250

1962 TOPPS "GEHRIG AND RUTH" #140

So powerful was the attraction of Babe Ruth that Topps, even 14 years after The Bambino's death, released a 10-card subset of Ruth in '62 called Babe Ruth Special. Interestingly, this card from that subset features a shot from Lou Gehrig Day in Yankee Stadium in 1939. After Gehrig's speech to the crowd in which he said he considered himself "the luckiest man on the face of the earth," Ruth rushed over to him and gave him this bear hug, thus ending a celebrated feud between the two men. Believe it, this was an important and healing moment in The Babe's life. And this card provides collectors with a dual card of the two men who formed the heart of Murder's Row.

$25–$50

1962 TOPPS "MANAGER'S DREAM" MANTLE/MAYS #18

"And the winner of the most appropriately named card ever is . . ."

$125–$200

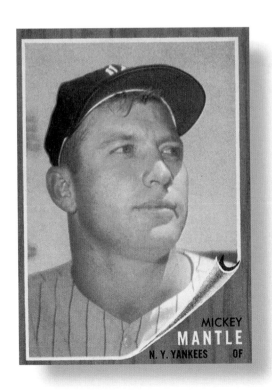

1962 TOPPS MICKEY MANTLE #200

This is how The Mick looked in his final MVP season, which included a .321 average, 30 home runs, 89 RBI and a league-leading 122 walks. It also included a stint of about a month on the disabled list in May, when he tore his hamstring in one leg and ligaments in the other sprinting out an infield hit. When he returned, he returned swinging, and the Yankees cruised to a World Series championship over the San Francisco Giants.

$350–$450

1962 TOPPS JOE TORRE #218

Even back in '62, Joe was a cool customer. Hat backward, two hands steadying that large pancake of a glove and generally ready for anything the Topps photographer could throw his way. Today, for as good a manager as Torre has been with the New York Yankees (he's led the Bronx Bombers to World Series titles in 1996 and 1998), he was also a decent player. Did we say decent? Actually, there are some comparisons to make between Torre and Mickey Mantle. Both played 18 years, both finished with exactly 344 doubles, both finished with almost the same batting average (Mantle .298, Torre .297) and both finished within 73 hits of each other. Both were also MVP winners, Mantle three times and Torre in 1971 when he batted .363-24-137 with the St. Louis Cardinals. All of this isn't to suggest that Joe Torre was another Mickey Mantle — he wasn't. Rather, we make these observations only to let the world know that Joe Torre was a pretty darn good ballplayer.

$25–$40

1962 POST ROGER MARIS #6

From 1960 through 1963, boxes of Post Cereal included cards on the boxes for collectors to cut out. A regular size family box of cereal included eight cards on the box, providing a decent start to a set. The "61" on this card pops out almost as much as the signature of Roger Maris, who boldly signed the card long after its release.

$15–$25

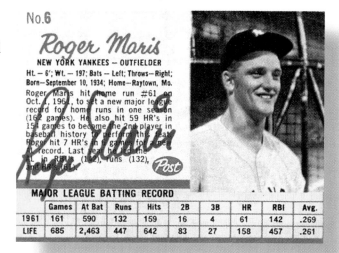

1962 TOPPS WILLIE MAYS #300

Even though both the Dodgers and Giants had moved to California several seasons earlier, the rivalry remained intense. In 1962, Mays played in all 162 games, batted .304, whacked a league-leading 49 home runs, drove in 141 RBI and had his best season in center field, committing his fewest errors ever (four). All of that helped the Giants tie the Dodgers for first place on the final day of the season and slip past L.A. in a three-game playoff for the NL pennant. The Giants ultimately lost to the Yankees in Game 7 of the World Series, but without Mays, they never would have had a chance to tie their dreaded rivals, dispose of them, and then take the World Series to the limit.

$80–$150

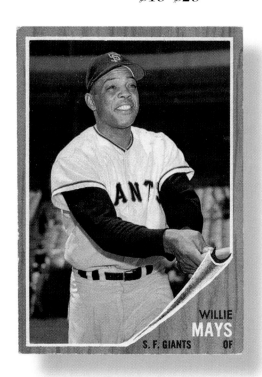

1962 TOPPS LOU BROCK #387

This must be painful for Cubs fans. Lou Brock could have been wearing a Cubs uniform en route to the Hall of Fame, but instead was a member of the rival St. Louis Cardinals, compliments of an ill-advised six-player deal Chicago made to acquire pitcher Ernie Broglio (along with pitcher Bobby Shantz and outfielder Doug Clemens). In 2$^{1}/_{2}$ seasons with the Cubs, Broglio went a combined 7–19. Shantz was 12–10 before being sent back to the Cardinals and finally the Phillies, and Clemens hit .221 with four homers in his only full season in Chicago. Brock went on to steal more bases than any other player in major league history (938, since broken by Rickey Henderson) and collected more than 3,000 hits — no doubt many of those steals and hits coming at Wrigley against the Cubs. No, it can't be easy being a Cubbie fan.

$75–$125

1962 TOPPS "MARIS BLASTS 61ST" #313

Straight stride, head down, arms extended, hips turned. Roger was picture perfect on this card, which includes his complete minor and major league stats on the back.

$25–$40

1963 TOPPS STAN MUSIAL #250

Musial's final regular-issue baseball card was released during his final season, and thus does not contain complete major league stats. (He played the entire 1963 season.) But it's an important issue in the Musial card library, and it provided card collectors and fans their last look at the greatest player in Cardinals history. Stan the Man retired at the age of 42.

$75–$125

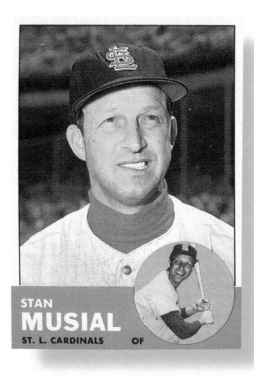

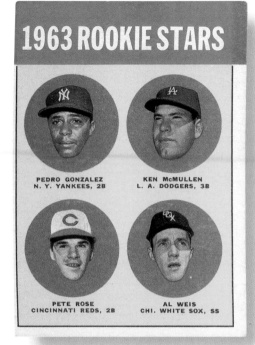

1963 TOPPS "1963 ROOKIE STARS" (PETE ROSE) #537

The little guy in the lower left did, indeed, end up a star just like the card advertised. There was a time when Pete Rose was just a hustling ballplayer with a really atrocious haircut. But he fashioned a 23-year career that saw him finish as the major league's all-time hit king (4,256) and brought into vogue the headfirst slide. Does Pete's lifetime banishment from baseball for allegedly betting on baseball while managing the Cincinnati Reds diminish this card? Probably not. This card was one of the hobby's first to enjoy a boom from speculative interest. Besides, 4,256 hits are a lot of hits. Rose was an important player to the game, and this is an important card to the baseball card hobby.

$500–$850

1964 TOPPS "TOPS IN NL" (AARON/MAYS) #423

Tops in NL? How about tops in big-league history. These two combined for 1,415 home runs (Aaron 755, No. 1 all-time; Mays 660, No. 3 all-time). That's a lot of souvenir baseballs rattling around the bleachers.

$75–$125

1964 TOPPS CASEY STENGEL #324

In 1958, the Senate Subcommittee on Anti-Trust and Monopoly — looking to recognize baseball's exemption — hauled Casey Stengel in front of the committee. Chairman Estes Kefauver, the honorable senator from Tennesee, was the chairman and called Casey as the first witness. When Kefauver asked Casey his views on the legislation, he and the committee got pure classic Stengel wisdom in return.

This is what the committee heard:

"I would say I would not know, but I would say the reason they want it passed is to keep baseball going as the highest paid ball sport that has gone into baseball, and from the baseball angle — I am not going to speak of any other sport. I am not in here to argue about these other sports. I am in the baseball business. It has been run cleaner than any business that has ever put out in the one hundred years at the present time."

That's part of Casey's testimony, verbatim. As Casey himself would have said, "You could look it up."

$8–$15

1965 TOPPS "MANTLE'S CLUTCH HR" #134

We have no scientific data to serve as proof, but we're going to take a guess that of all of Mickey's 536 career home runs in the regular season, and 18 homers in the World Series, nearly half of them fell under the heading of "clutch." His three homers against the Cardinals in the '64 World Series were the last Series home runs Mantle hit.

$45–$70

1965 TOPPS "CARDS ROOKIES" (STEVE CARLTON) #477

This Rookie Card of Lefty hails from the semi-high series in 1965, a series which several hobbyists believe is tougher to locate cards from than the highest series. Topps sometimes hit and sometimes missed with its rookie prospects — much like card companies today. Here's a big hit. Carlton would go on to win 329 games and collect more than 4,000 strikeouts. Nice call, Topps.

$125–$225

1965 TOPPS "1965 ROOKIE STARS" (JOE MORGAN) #16

This Rookie Card pictures Little Joe with the old Houston Colt 45s, but Morgan made his name with back-to-back NL MVP awards with Cincinnati's Big Red Machine in 1975 and '76. Morgan possessed a rare combination of speed and power for a second baseman, and the Reds won back-to-back world championships with Joe hitting in the third spot in the powerful Reds lineup. This card is a double print, but remains the most valuable card in the 1965 1st Series.

$40–$70

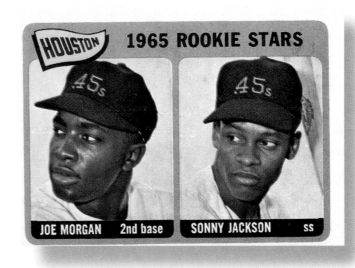

1965 TOPPS "ATHLETICS ROOKIES" (JIM "CATFISH" HUNTER) #526

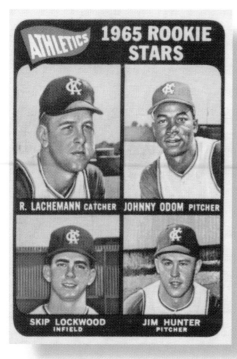

All four players on this high-series short-print Rookie Card logged time in the major leagues, but only Jim Hunter played his way into the Hall of Fame. The native of North Carolina actually made his major league debut a year after the release of this card. But we know that Hunter went on to win 224 major league games, compile a 5–3 record in six World Series (three with Oakland, three with the New York Yankees), sign a $3.5 million free-agent contract with the Yankees in 1975 (which at the time was the largest sum ever paid to a player), hurl a perfect game for the A's and get inducted into the Baseball Hall of Fame in 1987. We know all that, but Topps clearly had no idea the greatness that awaited Hunter. The company misspelled his name "Tim" on the card back and never corrected it.

$50–$80

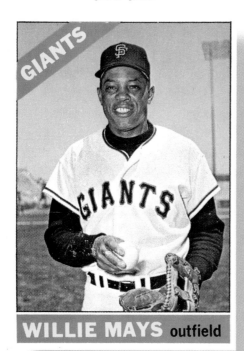

1966 TOPPS SANDY KOUFAX #100

Sandy Koufax went out on top. There was no hanging on, no jumping from team to team, no banishment to the bullpen in an effort to recapture lost skills. Koufax never lost his skills, period, and probably could have put up bigger numbers had he had not retired at the age of 30. In 1966, his final season in the big leagues, Koufax was absolutely amazing, winning 27 games. He also led the NL with five shutouts, 323 innings pitched, a 1.79 ERA and 317 strikeouts. He led the NL in strikeouts four seasons, with 300-plus whiffs coming in three of those. He was in a class by himself, then he walked away. This was his last card, released in the 1st Series.

$40–$75

1966 TOPPS WILLIE MAYS #1

Mays' 37 home runs and 103 RBI in 1966 represented the last time The Say Hey Kid said hello to the 30 home run/100 RBI mark. He also turned in another outstanding season in center field, winning the 10th of his 12 consecutive Gold Glove awards. Mays, at 35, was No. 1 in Giants fans' hearts and No. 1 in the '66 Topps set.

$75–$150

1966 Topps Roger Maris #365

This is the last Yankees card of the player who provided the New York club with two consecutive MVP seasons and a single-season home run mark that stood 37 years before being broken by both Mark McGwire and Sammy Sosa. That 37-year span represented the longest period of time any player has ever held the single-season home run mark. A blank-backed "proof" of a 1967 Topps Maris card listing him as a member of the Yankees surfaced with the release of the 1967 cards, but it's not a regular card. This is the last of the true pinstripe issues for Maris.

$25–$40

1966 Topps Jim Palmer #126

It's tough to say what Palmer is best known for. He won three Cy Young awards, often feuded with Earl Weaver, his manager in Baltimore, won 20 or more games eight times, posed for underwear advertisements, posted World Series victories in three different decades and was enshrined into the Hall of Fame. He also threw strikes, but we guess you figured that one out by now.

$60–$100

1967 Topps Whitey Ford #5

The Yankee Dynasty might have been over by 1967, but some of the best players were still in the game. At this point in his career, Whitey Ford was fighting injuries and had even worked as an official and unofficial pitching coach for the Yankees. More than anything else, Whitey was a winner. And this card — his last — carries nearly complete career statistics, showing Ford as competitive right to the end.

$10–$20

1967 TOPPS MICKEY MANTLE #150

This is a great card, picturing the most popular player in the game at the time coupled with the popular design of the 1967 set. This is also the last card to list The Mick as an outfielder; he moved to first base to ease the pain in his injury-ravaged knees.

$200–$300

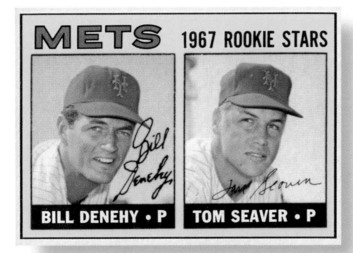

1967 TOPPS "METS ROOKIE STARS" (TOM SEAVER) #581

The New York Metropolitans had been the welcome mat of the rest of the National League since their arrival into the league in 1962. But the arrival of Tom Seaver in 1967 changed the franchise's fortunes, and provided the club with a true star to pin its future on. In 1967, no one knew that future was just two years away. This Seaver Rookie Card is an extremely tough find in the '67 high-number series.

$450–$850

1967 TOPPS "AL ROOKIE STARS" (ROD CAREW) #569

There's no telling if Topps had planned a Carew card for 1967, but after the rookie came out swinging the bat, the cardmaker certainly got one out in the high-number series. Carew's .292–8–51 effort with seven triples in '67 earned him 19 of the 20 votes for AL Rookie of the Year (with the lone non-Carew vote going to Reggie Smith of Boston). Carew went on to collect 3,053 hits as a member of the Minnesota Twins and California Angels and was elected to the Hall of Fame in 1991, his first year of eligibility. This card is a double print, making it available to a few more collectors than it normally would have been.

$125–$225

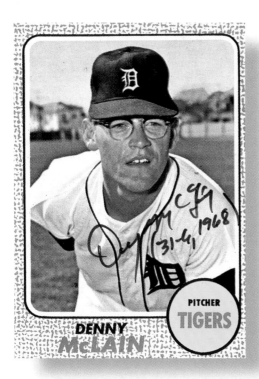

1968 TOPPS DENNY MCLAIN #40

" . . .with eyes 20/20, was nearsighted Denny, won all of the baseball awards." Those words are from a song about McLain crafted during the 1968 season and played on local Detroit radio. While making history with a 31-6 mark that season, McLain stopped to wallow in the celebrity. Tommy Smothers had McLain out to his house, Glen Campbell stepped into the Tiger clubhouse to hang out and Ed Sullivan booked McLain as a guest on his immensely popular variety show. All the while, McLain kept winning games. When he won his 30th game of the season, Dizzy Dean, the last pitcher to win 30 in a season, was on hand, as was Sandy Koufax, who was working the game for NBC. More celebrity. Regardless of what his teammates thought of McLain — and there are varying reports of that — it was Denny who led the club to the AL pennant and the World Series. And for that wonderful season, it was Denny who was the entertainer, and it was Denny who won all of the baseball awards.

$5–$10

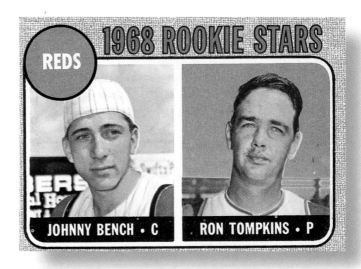

1968 TOPPS "1968 ROOKIE STARS" (JOHNNY BENCH) #247

Very few players throughout history can lay claim to having revolutionized the game. Johnny Bench can. Johnny Bench changed the way catchers played the position, and his contributions are still being felt today, including catchers catching with their right arm tucked behind their back. Bench's arm was legendary, and he could gun a would-be base stealer out at second base without ever leaving his crouch. Bench brought defense to the forefront for catchers, and he combined that with poise and power at the plate as well. It certainly wasn't a stretch for Topps to include the confident looking young catcher on a Rookie Stars card, and Bench proved Topps wise by winning the 1968 NL Rookie of the Year Award.

$75–$125

1968 TOPPS "1968 ROOKIE STARS" (NOLAN RYAN) #177

There was a time in the hobby when this was referred to as the "Jerry Koosman Rookie Card." These days, it's not likely even Mrs. Koosman calls it Jerry's Rookie Card. That's no disrespect to Koosman, who won 222 games in the major leagues. But Nolan Ryan — the high-hat wearing cowboy on the right — has the strikeouts (5,714), the no-hitters (seven) and the Hall of Fame plaque to earn the right to call this Rookie Card his own.

$600–$900

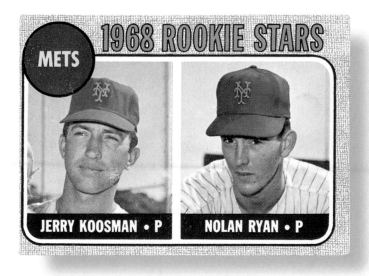

1968 TOPPS BOB GIBSON #100

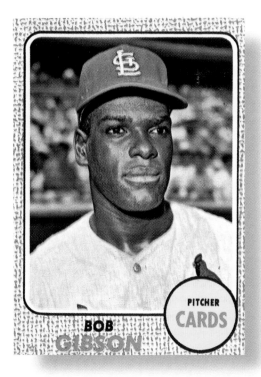

In The Year of the Pitcher, Gibson might very well have been the pitcher of the year. While Denny McLain went 31-6 with a 1.96 ERA that same season in the American League, Gibson turned in what has to rank as one of the most dominant seasons ever recorded by a pitcher. He fashioned a 22–9 mark that included:
• a 15-game consecutive win streak
• an incredible stretch where he allowed just two runs through 92 innings
• an NL-leading 268 strikeouts in 304-2/3 innings
• a major league-leading 13 shutouts
• 28 complete games
• just 62 walks
• a major league-leading 1.12 ERA, still the lowest ERA of any pitcher in the 20th century who threw at least 300 innings.

Almost doesn't seem fair, does it.

$13–$25

1969 TOPPS JOHNNY BENCH #95

The glove in this '69 1st Series card is made of leather, but for 10 consecutive seasons (1968–77) Bench walked away with Gold Gloves.

$30–$45

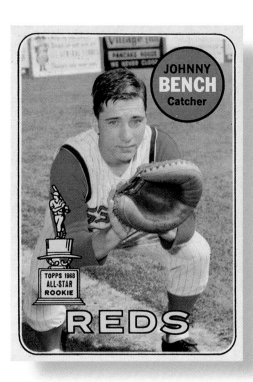

Bob Gibson yielded only 5 hits as he tamed the Tigers. His 17 strikeouts passed Sandy Koufax' old mark of 15.

1969 Topps "1968 World Series Game 1" (Bob Gibson) #162

If the Detroit Tigers didn't know much about Bob Gibson before Game 1 of the '68 World Series, they knew more than they wanted by the end of the game. At one point in the game, Gibson fanned Al Kaline, Norm Cash, Willie Horton, Jim Northrup and Bill Freehan (the No. 3-7 hitters) consecutively, mixing a deadly curveball with a fastball that the Tigers could barely even foul off. Horton said Gibson threw "as hard in the ninth inning as he did in the first." This World Series subset card features a headline that still holds today, as no pitcher has broken Gibson's record 17 strikeouts in a World Series game.

$4–$8

1969 Topps Tom Seaver #480

Tom was Terrific in 1969, and the Miracle Mets were the beneficiaries. Seaver's 25 wins and 2.21 ERA earned him the first of his three Cy Young awards, and helped earn the Mets a most improbable World Series victory. You want a '69 Mets card? This one is, shall we say, terrific.

$40–$70

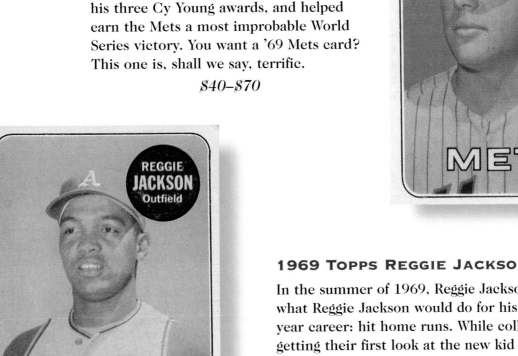

1969 Topps Reggie Jackson #260

In the summer of 1969, Reggie Jackson was doing what Reggie Jackson would do for his entire 21-year career: hit home runs. While collectors were getting their first look at the new kid in Oakland on this card, Reggie was hitting home runs in bunches. By the end of July, he had already slugged 40. Reggie only hit seven more homers that season, but the baseball world had officially been introduced to one of the game's premier sluggers (563 career home runs) and entertaining personalities.

$175–$275

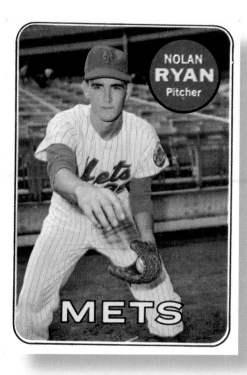

1969 TOPPS MICKEY MANTLE (WHITE LETTER) #500B

Variations on baseball cards are an accepted part of the hobby. But a variation on a Mickey Mantle card? What's up with that? One has to wonder what was going on at the Topps printing facility when the company was printing cards from the 5th Series. A group of players have their last name printed in white rather than the yellow it was supposed to be printed in. Bring on the conspiracy theorists, as one of the white letter variations is Mantle, which just happens to be The Mick's last card and just happens to include complete career stats on the card back. Whatever happened, the white letter variation is a tough issue to find. Both versions of the '69 Mantle carry the same message on the back: "Mickey announced his retirement from baseball on March 1, 1969."

$500–$1,000

1969 TOPPS TED WILLIAMS #650

A high-numbered card in the final 1969 series, and a card in which it appears the play of his Washington Senators wasn't so Splendid for The Splinter that day.

$10–$20

1969 TOPPS NOLAN RYAN #533

This is the first card picturing Nolan by himself, and it looks like the newest Hall of Famer is reaching out to touch the photographer. After all, he didn't just pitch the ball, as we can clearly see the ball in his glove. This is also the card many collectors turned to when The Express' 1968 Rookie Card rolled up in price.

$200–$400

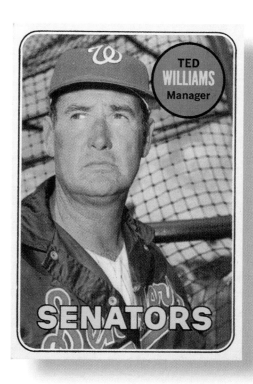

The backdrop of the 1970s, from a baseball perspective, would have to be Hank Aaron's 715th home run in 1974, the shot that made him baseball's all-time home run king. Unfortunately, the rest of the backdrop would have to be for something away from the field that dominated just as many headlines: free agency.

Free agency forced a change in the way fans looked at the game and its players. Suddenly, players who had performed admirably for the home team were labeled "traitor" and "greedy" for shopping their services to all interested clubs when their contracts were up.

Other baseball news of the '70s included the tragic death of Roberto Clemente, who died in a plane accident on the last day of 1972 trying to shuttle aid to the people of Managua, Nicaragua, who had been devastated by an earthquake that killed some 10,000 people. Jackie Robinson also

REGGIE JACKSON

RIVERFRONT STADIUM

HANK AARON

passed away during the decade, as did Yankees catcher and captain Thurman Munson who — like Clemente — died tragically when the plane he was piloting crashed near his Ohio home during the 1979 season.

In other headlines: Ohio national guardsmen shot and killed four students at Kent State University during an anti-war protest in 1970, the Beatles said "Let it Be" and disbanded, the Watergate affair started with the arrest of five burglars at Democratic Headquarters and ended with the resignation of President Richard M. Nixon, Elvis Presley died, George Lucas directed "Star Wars," and Frank Robinson became the major leagues' first African-American manager.

Baseball cards changed somewhat during the decade. Topps tried to keep up with the changing times with a mod design in 1972, then discontinued the release of cards in series by releasing the entire set all at once beginning in 1974. The decade also saw the final regular issue cards of Willie Mays and Hank Aaron, among many others.

JOHNNY BENCH

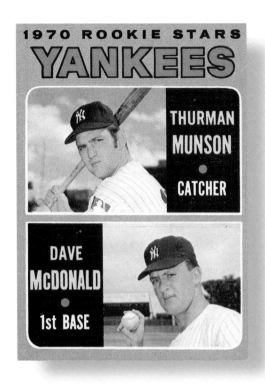

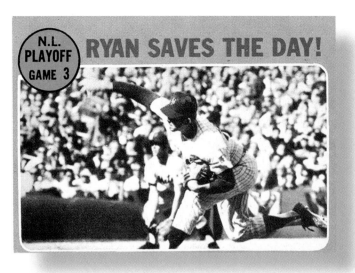

1970 Topps Thurman Munson #189

Fans of baseball in the 1970s certainly remember the New York Yankees' captain. Munson was the heart and soul of the club, and was the leader on the field and in the clubhouse during the Yanks' dynasty later in the decade. He played hurt, and he played hard. While collectors were getting their first look at Munson on this card, the catcher was doing quite well in the major leagues. He finished 1970 with a .302 average, 25 doubles and American League Rookie of the Year honors.

$30–$50

1970 Topps "Ryan Saves the Day" #197

Before Nolan Ryan was Nolan Ryan: Hall of Famer, he was Nolan Ryan: relief pitcher for the New York Mets. He started a few games for the Mets in 1969, but he worked out of the bullpen a little more frequently. It was during one of those relief appearances that Ryan provided a sign of greatness to come. Entering Game 3 of the Mets' NL Championship Series against the Braves with the Mets trailing 2-0, Nolan — then 22 — worked seven innings of relief, striking out seven and winning the deciding game, to help send the Amazin' Mets to the World Series. One other note: Nolan also did it with the bat that day, going 2-for-4 and scoring a run. Topps' headline writers were right; Ryan, indeed, had saved the day.

$15–$30

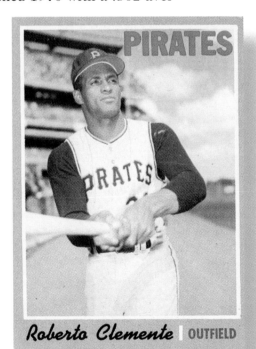

1970 Topps Roberto Clemente #350

By 1970, Roberto Clemente was recognized as one of the most gifted players in the game. A post-season appearance in the 1970 NL Championship Series further highlighted Clemente to the world, as did his play in the World Series the next season. This card, not part of any difficult series, still ranks among the top four in value in the 1970 set.

$35–$70

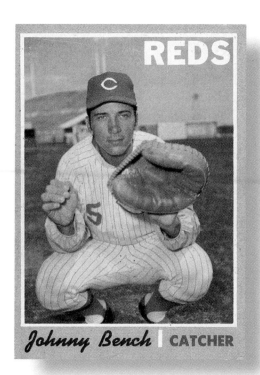

Johnny Bench | CATCHER

Hank Aaron | OUTFIELD

1970 TOPPS JOHNNY BENCH #660

It may come as a surprise to many that this third-year Bench card is almost as valuable as the Hall of Famer's Rookie Card. What, you say? See, Johnny got stuck in the high-number series in 1970, where even the most common of commons can run as much as a $10 bill for a Mint copy. So when you consider that Bench — as far from common status as they come — resides in the high rent district, where lesser quantities of cards were produced, you begin to see the reasoning.

$50–$100

1970 TOPPS HANK AARON #500

It was right about the time this 1970 card of The Hammer was released that Hank not only collected his 3,000th hit, but he also began drawing attention as a legitimate threat to Babe Ruth's career home run mark. As card #500, Topps certainly held Aaron in high regard and recognized his talent. That was a special number, held for super-star-caliber players. The previous year had seen Mickey Mantle given the honor of card #500.

$30–$50

1971 TOPPS THURMAN MUNSON #5

Topps got a little inventive in 1971, introducing game-action shots on the fronts of many cards. This is one of the better photos of Munson, and captures him doing what he did best: getting down and dirty.

$9–$18

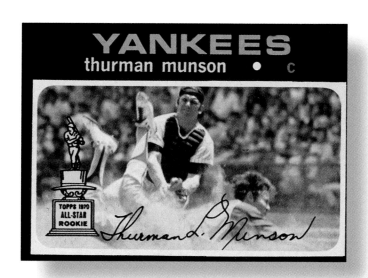

DODGERS
steve garvey • 3rd base

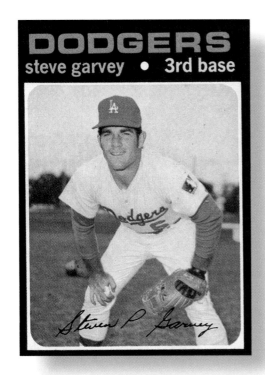

1971 TOPPS STEVE GARVEY #341

When we think of Steve Garvey, we think of him as part of baseball's longest-running infield. But that was as a first baseman with the Dodgers, not as a third baseman, as this Garvey Rookie Card clearly labels him. The switch of corners was made when Garvey's throws from third were, shall we say, a bit adventuresome. The move suited Garvey fine, and he won four Gold Gloves and retired with a fielding average of .996 at the position. Throwing down to second base could sometimes be a challenge, but what the heck, Garvey had found his place. He also found himself on 10 All-Star Teams, and by the end of '74, had earned the National League MVP Award. Yes sir, first base suited Garvey just fine.

$18–$30

CUBS
ernie banks • 1st base

1971 TOPPS ERNIE BANKS #525

This is Mr. Cub's last card as an active player, as Banks retired after 39 games in 1971 — his legs tired, but his spirit still fresh. His 47 home runs in 1958 is still a record for a

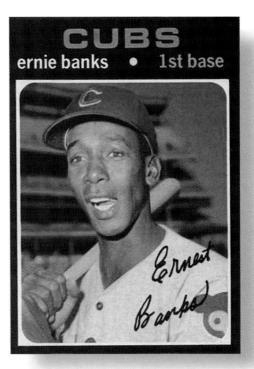

shortstop, and he's a member of the 500 Home Run Club. Although he never played in a World Series in his 19 years, Banks still remained an upbeat ambassador for baseball. "What a great day for baseball," Banks once said. "Let's play two." Like all '71 cards, this is susceptible to chipping because of the black borders. It's also a part of the semi-high series, making it a little more difficult to find than early-series releases.

$30–$50

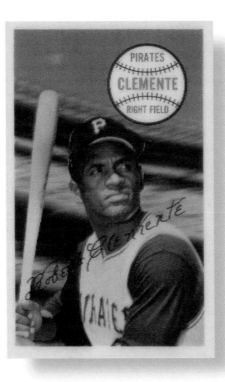

1970 KELLOGG'S ROBERTO CLEMENTE #27

Putting cards on cereal boxes was an old concept by 1970, but putting cards inside boxes of cereal — away somewhere in the middle of the Frosted Flakes and Rice Krispies — was fairly new. And collectors in 1970 ate it up. This 3-D Clemente card fell right between #'s 16–30, which many veteran dealers believe are in shorter supply than the rest of the set.

$15–$30

1972 TOPPS "1972 ROOKIE STARS RED SOX" (CARLTON FISK) #79

Fisk was a four-decade player, having entered the league for two games in 1969. What's even more amazing is that Fisk was a four-decade catcher, which makes our knees hurt just thinking about it. Along the way, Fisk set the record for most games played as a catcher (2,229) and hit a dramatic 12th-inning, game-winning home run in Game 6 of the 1975 World Series against the Cincinnati Reds. This '72 Rookie Card captures the young Fisk, the one who legged out nine triples that season (tied for first in the AL) and was the first-ever unanimous selection as AL Rookie of the Year.

$30–$60

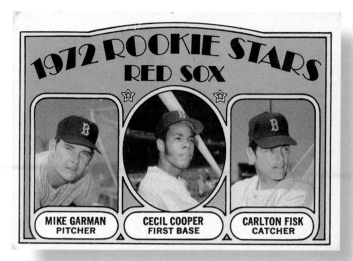

1972 TOPPS STEVE CARLTON "TRADED" #751

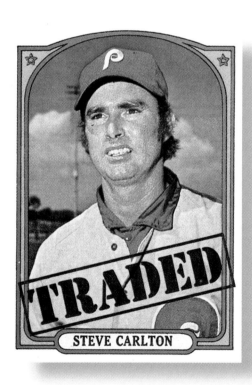

After the first three series of Topps' 1972 cards were completed, several trades involving big names were consummated, leaving the cardmaker with a bit of a situation on its hands. The solution: slap a printed "Traded" stamp across the front of a card picturing the player in his new uniform. In February of 1972, the Cardinals traded Steve Carlton to the Phillies for Rick Wise, a good-hitting pitcher. Regardless of the fact that the Cardinals hosed themselves with the deal — Carlton won the first of his four Cy Young awards that first season with the Phillies and Wise gave the Cards two solid years before he was traded again — the deal lives on for all to see and judge, thanks to Topps' Traded subset.

$30–$50

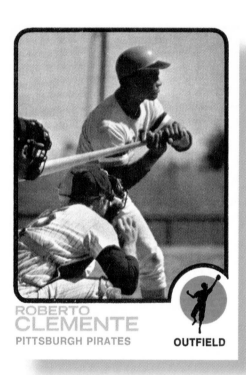

1973 TOPPS ROBERTO CLEMENTE #50

This is Clemente's final card, which features complete major league stats. The 3,000 hits line really sticks out on the back. This card, part of the 1st Series, likely was produced before Clemente's death on Dec. 31, 1972. Topps still released the card, but with no mention of the HOFer's untimely death.

$30–$70

1973 Topps Willie Mays #305

This is Willie Mays' last regular-issue base-ball card. Mays' first card pictures him in a New York uniform (Giants), and his last regular-issue card also pictures him in a New York uniform — only this one is the New York Mets, whom acquired the Say Hey Kid from San Francisco in May 1972. Although his once incomparable skills were eroding with age, Mays played the entire '73 season with the Mets, helping the club get to the World Series where they lost to the Oakland A's in seven games.

$20–$35

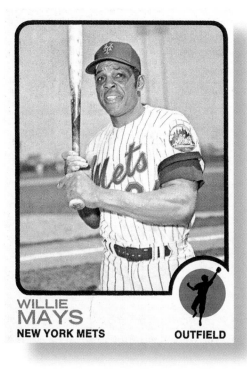

WILLIE
MAYS
NEW YORK METS   **OUTFIELD**

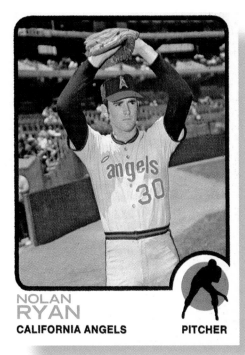

NOLAN
RYAN
CALIFORNIA ANGELS   **PITCHER**

1973 Topps Nolan Ryan #220

The 1973 season served notice to the base-ball world that Nolan Ryan was the real deal. Following his first 300-plus strikeout season in 1972, The Ryan Express hurled two no-hitters in two months and finished the season with a record 383 strikeouts. Look at Nolan's picture on this card; what could hitters have been thinking when he reached this part of his motion? Or could they even hear themselves think with their knees knocking?

$50–$90

1973 Topps "1973 Rookie Third Basemen" (Mike Schmidt) #615

The most prolific third baseman — and it ain't The Penguin or Hilton —resides on this Rookie Card. Michael Jack Schmidt, a first ballot Hall of Famer who is considered by many to be the best all-around third baseman ever, just happens to be on a short-printed Rookie Card. That only adds value to an already significant card.

$175–$300

1973 ROOKIE THIRD BASEMEN

RON
CEY
LOS ANGELES DODGERS

JOHN
HILTON
SAN DIEGO PADRES

MIKE
SCHMIDT
PHILADELPHIA PHILLIES

1974 TOPPS HANK AARON #1

If ever Topps went out on the limb, it was 1974. Well, it was a short, sturdy limb. Topps went ahead and printed "New All-Time Home Run King" on Hank Aaron's card in 1974, even though Aaron entered the '74 season still one home run away from tying Babe Ruth's mark and two blasts from passing it. The fact that Aaron hadn't yet passed Ruth as collectors were pulling this card out of packs seemed pretty irrelevant at the time. It was just a foregone conclusion that it would happen. Aaron didn't make the folks at Topps squirm much, as he tied Ruth with a home run on Opening Day. Then, just a few days later, Aaron broke the record with a nationally televised Monday Night blast off the Dodgers' Al Downing. And from that moment on, the '74 Topps card officially became accurate.

$20–$40

1974 TOPPS FRANK ROBINSON #55

Winding down his career in Southern California, Frank Robinson found himself in an unfamiliar role — fulltime designated hitter. The DH was brought to the American League in 1973 and seemed to be instituted specifically for Robby. At 38, and as a fulltime DH (127 games in that role, only 17 in the outfield), Robinson belted 30 home runs. He proved that older ballplayers could still hit, and had a place in the game. This is a historic card as it marks Topps' first card of a player ever listed as a DH.

$3–$6

1974 TOPPS NOLAN RYAN #20

By 1974, Topps finally issued its cards in one series. That solved distribution problems, but it couldn't do a thing for quality control. Some of the card sheets were still being miscut and thus several are found off-center. This Ryan card, still an early card in Nolan's career, is notorious for being off-center.

$35–$70

1974 TOPPS MIKE SCHMIDT #283

By the time he found himself pictured alone on a baseball card (he shared it with two others on his '73 Rookie Card), Michael Jack Schmidt was just trying to make sure there might be another card after this one. That wasn't a sure thing after a .196 batting average in his first full season in the big leagues, although that average did include 18 home runs. A funny thing happened during the '74 season, though: Schmidt hit, and hit a lot. He doubled his home run output to a league-leading 36 and nearly doubled his batting average to .282. He also was selected to his first All-Star Game in '74. So all in all, it was a good year for Schmidt to have on his own card. Furthermore, there was no doubt there would be more Schmidt cards in the future. He had seen to that.

$20–$40

1974 TOPPS WILLIE MCCOVEY "WASHINGTON NAT'L LEAGUE" #250B

It was a strong rumor, to be sure, but still it was only a rumor that the San Diego Padres would be relocated to Washington, D.C. for the 1974 season. But Topps went with the rumor, producing some "Washington" variations on select Padres cards. The move never happened, and Topps quickly corrected the Padres cards. The young hobby in 1974 jumped all over the variations, and this card of HOFer McCovey is the most popular.

$15–$30

1974 TOPPS DAVE WINFIELD #456

Winfield had a lot of choices coming out of the University of Minnesota in 1973. He was drafted by the NFL (despite not having played college football), NBA and the old ABA, but chose a baseball career instead after the Padres made him the fourth overall pick in 1973. He went directly to the major leagues without ever spending a day in the minors. He had his ups and downs in the major leagues. The ups: a World Series title with Toronto and some years with the Yankees. The downs: the accidental beaning of a flying seagull and some years with the Yankees (remember the moronic "Mr. May" moniker slapped on him?). The fact is Winfield could hit in any month of the year. He finished as a winner, a member of the 3,000 hit club and a first-ballot future Hall of Famer. So there.

$40–$80

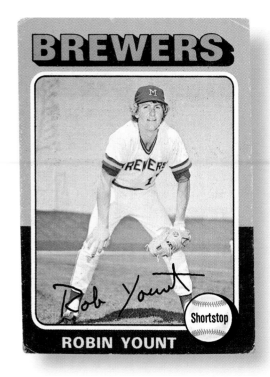

1975 TOPPS ROBIN YOUNT #223

Robin Yount and George Brett were a matched pair throughout their careers. Both finished their careers in 1993, and just 12 hits separated them. Both entered the Hall of Fame the same day and their 1975 Rookie Cards are just five numbers apart. But as a popular beer commercial noted during the summer of '99, Yount had multiple MVPs to Brett's one. One of Yount's MVP awards came as a shortstop, the other as a center fielder. This is a great card of Yount, then freshly out of high school.

$40–$80

1975 TOPPS GEORGE BRETT #228

At this time in his baseball career, there was absolutely nothing that indicated that George Brett would one day be George Brett. But by the time the 1975 season was over, and Brett had finished with a .308 average, this card was no longer considered just another Royals' common. Brett's three batting titles in three decades and his new HOF status have made this Rookie Card cardboard royalty.

$90–$150

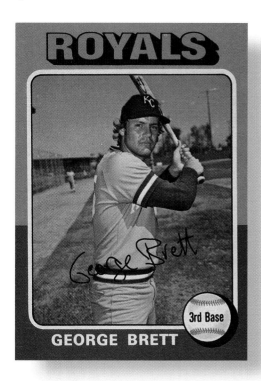

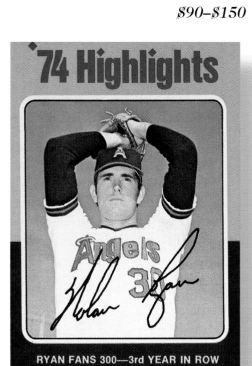

1975 TOPPS "RYAN FANS 300 – 3RD YEAR IN ROW" #5

After three straight seasons of fanning 300 or more batters, you would think a pitcher may hit the wall, like maybe for a lifetime. But not Nolan. He slowed to a more human-like 186 K's in 1975, then reeled off two more consecutive 300-plus strikeout seasons. He added another in 1989, at the tender age of 42. Is Ryan the best pitcher of all time? Probably not. Is he the greatest marvel as a pitcher ever? No doubt about it.

$20–$40

HERB WASHINGTON

1975 Topps Herb Washington #407

Former Oakland A's owner Charles O. Finley, the man who introduced orange baseballs for night play, mechanical rabbits to bring umpires baseballs and a mule for a mascot, thought he had outsmarted even himself in 1974 when he introduced the baseball world to Herb Washington. Who is Herb Washington? Only the first, and subsequently only, Designated Pinch Runner in major league history, that's who. Washington's job was to steal bases, and the former world class college track sprinter did his job well in '74, stealing 28 bases in the role of Designated Pinch Runner. But alas, the grand experiment failed when Washington was picked off first base in the World Series. He stole two bases in 13 games in 1975 before leaving baseball forever. He never set foot in the field or at the plate. Washington's final major league stats: 104 games, 30 stolen bases and one baseball card.

$1–$2

1975 Topps Harmon Killebrew #640

Topps issued this card of The Killer in 1975, but Killebrew never played for the Twins that season. Having been released after the '74 season — The Twins? Release Killebrew? — Harmon signed with the Kansas City Royals and played one final campaign. It was an unmemorable finish to a very memorable career. The happy ending came nine years later when Killebrew was elected to the Hall of Fame. Right there with the Hall of Fame in terms of thrills was "Harmon Killebrew Night" on "Late Night With David Letterman." The highlight that evening had to be when the late Liberace came out onstage and talked baseball with Harmon. Now that's entertainment!

$3–$5

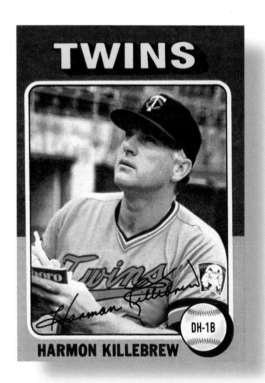

HARMON KILLEBREW

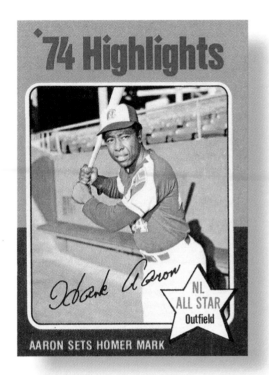

In what may have been the most anticipated card of the decade, Topps honored Hank Aaron for his record-breaking 715th home run. But wasn't an action shot from the actual event available?

$15–$30

1976 TOPPS HANK AARON #550

Even opponents of the designated hitter rule would have to admit that the DH allowed American League fans the opportunity to bid farewell to the game's all-time home run champ during the two seasons after he broke Babe Ruth's mark. The card of The Hammer, his last regular-issue Topps card, is also the only Aaron card with "Des. Hitter" as his position. That should come as a surprise to absolutely no one. It was Aaron, after all, who ably fit the role of designated superstar for 22 seasons.

$13–$25

1976 TOPPS KURT BEVACQUA "BUBBLE GUM BLOWING CHAMP" #564

Now here's an honest-to-goodness bubble gum card. Despite a decent major league career that included two home runs in the 1984 World Series, Bevacqua may best be remembered for dusting Johnny Oates in the championship round of Joe Garagiola's Bazooka Bubble Gum Blowing Tournament. Even if they don't remember the Series homers, Kurt, you've always got this.

$1–$2

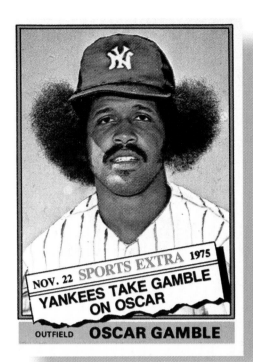

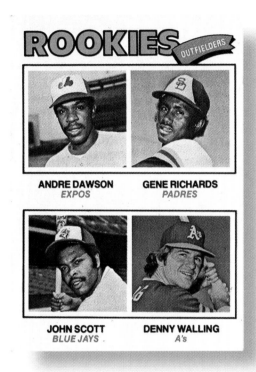

1976 TOPPS OSCAR GAMBLE #74T

Don't believe the hype; sometimes you *can* tell the players without a scorecard.

50 cents-$1

1977 TOPPS "ROOKIES OUTFIELDERS" (ANDRE DAWSON) #473

The Hawk fashioned a solid career that saw him win the 1977 Rookie of the Year Award, several Gold Gloves in right field and the NL MVP in 1987 when he slugged 49 homers. A good argument can be made that Dawson was the National League's best everyday player of the 1980s. With this card, you see where it all began.

$20–$40

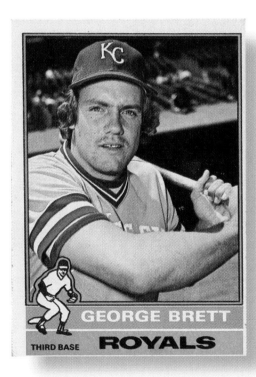

1976 TOPPS GEORGE BRETT #19

"They always seem to take those pictures at 8 o'clock in the morning," Brett once said of his baseball card photos. Well, here's a case where George clearly was right. This looks like a just-rolled-out-of-bed Brett the year he won his first batting title.

$30–$50

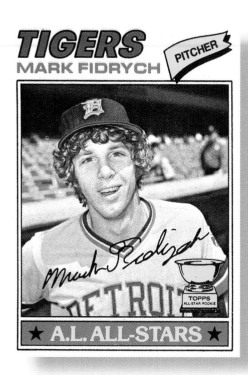

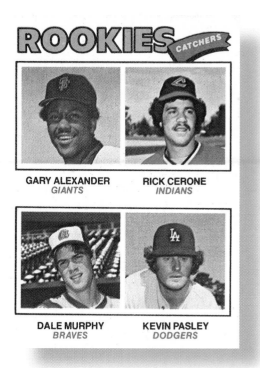

1977 TOPPS MARK FIDRYCH #265

The Bird was the Word during the Summer of '76, when Fidrych won 19 games as a rookie, led the league in ERA, started the All-Star Game and gave all of America a new appreciation for eccentricity. But what a bummer for collectors that summer to discover there was no Mark "The Bird" Fidrych card to be found during his reign atop the game. Topps already had issued its '76 set by the time Fidrych won his first game, and not surprisingly, Fidrych (who had spent the previous season in the minors) was not a part of it. Topps had to wait until the next year. When the '77 Topps cards finally rolled around, this is the one that led the way. This was the hot rookie, before there officially were hot rookies.

$2–$4

1977 TOPPS "ROOKIES CATCHERS" (DALE MURPHY) #476

The 1977 Topps Dale Murphy card is actually the first of two rookie-designated, four-player cards Murphy appears on. But although he's pictured on a four-player 1978 card as well, this is Dale's true Rookie Card. Fans who saw Murphy play remember him as a five-time Gold Glove winner in center field with the Braves. Center field is a long way from catcher, the position Murph actually played when he was signed, but — and this is hard to believe considering the Gold Gloves — his arm was so shaky that his throws back to the pitcher often sailed into center field. Yet he found a home in the outfield. At one point during the early 1980s, as the hobby boomed and Murphy won back-to-back MVP awards, this was one of the hottest baseball cards in the world.

$15–$30

1978 Topps Eddie Murray #36

Here, looking all business, is Eddie Murray. That business-like approach to the game helped him join Hank Aaron and Willie Mays as the only three players to slug 500 career home runs and collect 3,000 hits. And that feat alone makes this the most valuable card issued in Topps' 1978 set.

$40–$80

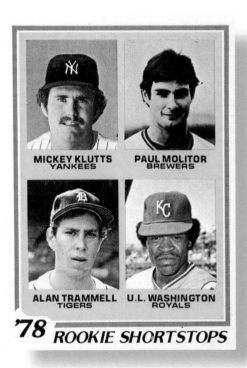

1979 Topps Ozzie Smith #116

The Wizard, before he was called the greatest defensive shortstop to ever play the game. This is a very difficult card to find perfectly centered.

$40–$80

1978 Topps "'78 Rookie Shortstops" (Paul Molitor/Alan Trammell) #707

Should both Molitor and Trammell find themselves elected to the Hall of Fame, this could be a card of distinction as the first Rookie Card ever to picture two HOFers. Molitor, a member of the 3,000 hit club, is a virtual lock. Trammell, with more than 2,300 hits, a World Series MVP Award and the distinction of being a member of the longest-running double-play combination ever, is a good bet.

$40–$80

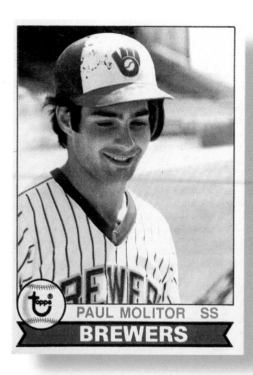

1979 TOPPS NOLAN RYAN #115

The final year of the decade also was Nolan's final year with the Angels. Of course, he went out as you would expect, leading the AL in strikeouts and shutouts. He also earned his first All-Star Game start in '79. After the season ended, Ryan signed a free-agent contract with the Houston Astros and became baseball's first $1-million-per-year player.

$15–$30

1979 TOPPS PAUL MOLITOR #24

After sharing a card the previous year, Molitor was awarded his own baseball card in '79. Placing Molly with a young Robin Yount in the infield provided the Brewers with instant credibility, and helped push them into serious contention during the next several seasons. (They claimed a World Series berth in 1982.) This card is rarely found perfectly centered and without print spots.

$8–$20

1979 TOPPS THURMAN MUNSON #310

During the summer of 1979, the unthinkable happened: Thurman Munson, the never-say-die Yankee, died in a horrible plane accident as the craft he was piloting crashed near his Canton, Ohio, home. Munson was the 1970s version of The Pride of the Yankees. In one of the great tributes of all time, the next time the Yankees took the field, home plate was left vacant, and the fans cheered in memory of Munson for several minutes. This card is the last issued of Munson as a player. And for many of us, it signaled the end of the '70s.

$1–$2

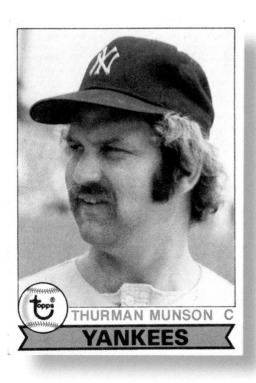

1980
1989

The baseball card floodgates opened in 1980 when a court order ruled in favor of Fleer and indicated that Topps did not have exclusive rights to produce and market baseball cards in packages with bubble gum. That brought both Fleer and Donruss into the market in 1981 to compete with Topps.

All three included gum in their packages, but that would be short-lived. A federal court ruled that Topps did in fact own exclusive rights to marketing baseball cards with bubble gum. Undaunted, Fleer simply packaged their cards with stickers while Donruss offered player puzzle pieces in their packs.

ROGER CLEMENS

Another set, called Score, was introduced to favorable reviews in 1988. And by the end of the decade, a new and upscale player, Upper Deck, entered the field and changed the look of cards with a higher per-pack price point, outstanding photos and a unique anti-counterfeiting hologram on the back of each card.

Topps released a boxed Traded Set from 1981 through the end of the decade, and the rest of the companies did the same with their sets in an effort to

DODGER STADIUM

release cards of significant traded players and rookies to an eager market.

On the field, the decade opened with George Brett making a serious run at the .400 mark. He fell just short, finishing at .390 but won the AL MVP Award and helped the Royals into the World Series where the club lost to the Philadelphia Phillies — the Phils' only World Series title.

Baltimore shortstop Cal Ripken took the field in 1982 and did not miss a game again until he sat himself out late in the 1998 season — an incredible streak of 2,632 games that covered 16 years. In 1984, the Detroit Tigers jumped out to a 35–5 mark in their first 40 games and coasted to a World Series championship. The New York Mets came from behind to defeat the Boston Red Sox in the 1986 World Series, and the Dodgers, backed by a game-winning, pinch-hit home run off the bat of Kirk Gibson in Game 1, downed the heavily-favored Oakland A's in the 1988 Fall Classic.

GEORGE BRETT

Tragedy struck during the 1989 World Series, when an earthquake in the Bay Area halted Game 3 of the Series between the San Francisco Giants and the Oakland A's. The Series was put on hold 10 days. Other baseball news from '89 included Reds manager Pete Rose's lifetime banishment from baseball for allegedly gambling on major league games, and the death of Commissioner Bart Giamatti shortly after making the Rose ruling.

In national headlines, the world mourned the death of John Lennon and the seven aboard the Space Shuttle Challenger, which exploded shortly after launch in 1986. The decade also brought the world the introduction of CNN, USA Today and the musical compact disc.

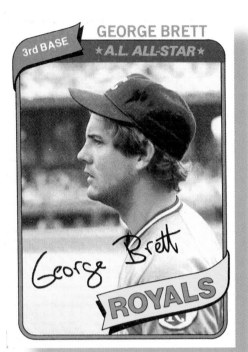

1980 TOPPS RICKEY HENDERSON #482

Here's the card of the greatest leadoff hitter and top base stealer in the history of the game. Henderson has set the standard for stolen bases, both in a single season and career. This is a difficult card to find in Mint condition, as many were handled and traded during the early 1980s when Ricky was running wild on the base paths. Perfectly centered copies are few and far between as well.

$35–$65

1980 TOPPS GEORGE BRETT #450

Sometimes, ballplayers hit the field in April and discover early on that it's just going to be their year. Denny McLain learned it in 1968, Steve Carlton and Rod Guidry learned it in 1972 and 1978, respectively. Mark McGwire and Sammy Sosa both learned it in 1998 as the nation watched their home run battle unfold. And George Brett learned it in 1980. Make no mistake; George Brett owned 1980. By August, Brett was hitting .400, and, suddenly, he was finding himself on the nightly news. Did Brett get a hit? Can he hit .400? Can anyone? Even through a rash of injuries, Brett battled and strung together a 37-game hitting streak. He finished the season at .390-24-118, the highest batting average by a third baseman this century.

$5–$12

1981 TOPPS "DODGERS FUTURE STARS" (FERNANDO VALENZUELA) #302

Fernandomania and Rookiemania. This was the most talked about, bought, sold and traded card in 1981, and it ushered in the Rookie Card craze almost single-handedly.

$1–$3

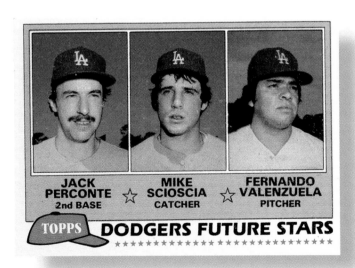

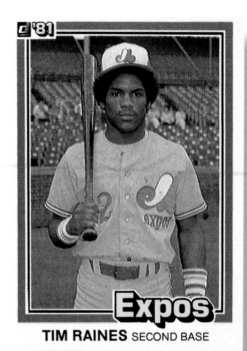

TIM RAINES SECOND BASE

BEST HITTERS

1981 DONRUSS TIM RAINES #538

Having missed by not including Fernando Valenzuela in its premiere baseball card set, Donruss could take solace in the addition of a Tim Raines card — the only Raines card picturing him alone and available to collectors until Topps included him in its Traded set near the end of the season. Raines was one of the few bright spots in a hastily produced set that included thin-as-skin paper stock, murky photography and printing flaws that made everyone look a little sunburned.

$1–$2

1981 DONRUSS "BEST HITTERS" (GEORGE BRETT/ROD CAREW) #537

Donruss, with their first baseball set, took a page from Topps and issued this multi-player card of George Brett and Rod Carew. With 10 batting titles between them, we'd say the card title is accurate.

60 cents–$1.50

1982 TOPPS TRADED OZZIE SMITH #109T

The Wizard makes his first appearance as a St. Louis Cardinal, the organization he'll always be linked with as the greatest defensive shortstop ever.

$10–$20

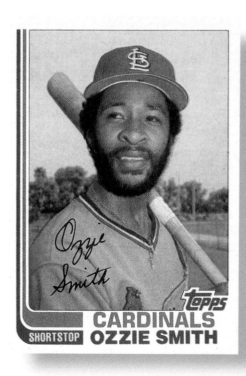

CARDINALS
SHORTSTOP **OZZIE SMITH**

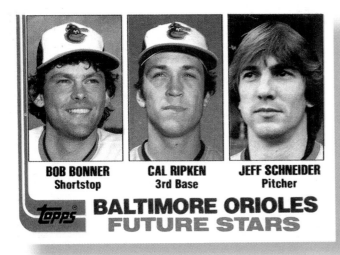

BOB BONNER
Shortstop

CAL RIPKEN
3rd Base

JEFF SCHNEIDER
Pitcher

BALTIMORE ORIOLES FUTURE STARS

1982 Topps "Baltimore Orioles Future Stars" (Cal Ripken Jr.) #21

All three of these players made it to the major leagues; some stayed a little longer than others. Only one — the guy in the middle — lived up to, and perhaps surpassed, the "Future Star" label.

$40–$60

1982 Topps Traded Cal Ripken Jr. #98T

What a great looking card. Check out the blue sky and green grass behind Cal. And does Rip look ready to hit, or what? This card became one of the first non-designated Rookie Cards to surpass a previously released RC in value. And it didn't just pass it, it blew by it, as this Traded card was in fewer quantities due to it initially only being available in the complete Traded boxed set.

$130–$200

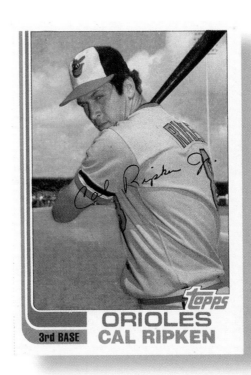

3rd BASE

ORIOLES CAL RIPKEN

Cal Ripken, Jr.
ORIOLES • THIRD BASE

1982 Fleer Cal Ripken Jr. #176

In July of 1982, Orioles manager Earl Weaver made a change to his lineup that would have a lasting impression on the Baltimore organization. He shifted Cal Ripken Jr. from third base to shortstop, where Ripken remained until 1997, helping redefine the position as one where big men with power can be every bit as graceful as the smaller, good-glove no-hit types.

$25–$40

1982 DONRUSS CAL RIPKEN JR. #405

Calvin Edwin Ripken Jr. may not be the best shortstop ever to come along, but he's close. His consecutive games played mark will stand for years — if not for all time. This much is for sure: This is one of the three '82 Rookie Cards of one of the classier, kinder and most gifted gentlemen ever to step onto a major league field.

$25–$40

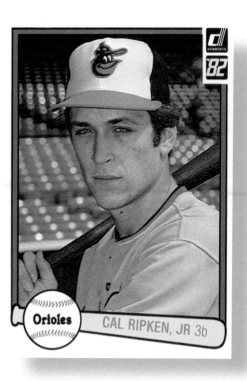

1983 TOPPS TONY GWYNN #482

Looks like a hit to left at Wrigley Field for Gwynn on this Rookie Card. Note Tony's uniform number; this was before he began wearing his familiar No. 19 jersey. This is one of three different Gwynn Rookie Cards, but helped with Topps' long tradition with collectors, it's the most valuable.

$35–$65

1983 TOPPS RYNE SANDBERG #83

Dallas Green, after being fired from the Phillies and hired by the Cubs, made sure that he picked up in trade a minor leaguer in the Phils' organization who caught his eye. And Green got his man in the deal, bringing Ryne Sandberg to the Windy City. Since Ryno came up to the big leagues before the days of nailing down any rookie at the earliest possible opportunity, he slipped through the cracks and was not a part of the 1982 Topps Traded set. So Sandberg made his card debut in 1983, appearing in all three major card manufacturer's sets. This Topps card is the most sought after of the three. Great player? You bet. Great card? Absolutely.

$10–$20

Tony Gwynn
OUTFIELD

1983 FLEER TONY GWYNN #360

No player in the 30-year history of the San Diego Padres is linked to the club more than Tony Gwynn, who has spent his entire 18-year major league career with the club. That's a rarity in this day and age of free agency. How good a hitter is Gwynn? At age 37 in 1997, he established career highs in doubles (49), homers (17) and RBI (119). And if you think he did it at the expense of his batting average, think again: He finished with the second-highest mark of his career at .372. Few players can produce a peak power season without a drop-off in average. But few players have the immense baseball skill of Tony Gwynn.

$18–$30

1983 TOPPS WADE BOGGS #498

As he chases his 3,000th career hit, interest in this card will again pick up. At the time of its release in '83, this is one of the cards collectors homed in on during an investment phase in the card hobby, mostly because Boggs' .349 average as a rookie in 1982 caught a lot of manufacturers' and speculators' attention. While this card enjoyed elite status that summer, so, too, did Wade who led the AL with a .361 batting average.

$13–$25

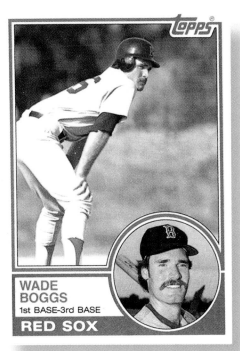

WADE BOGGS
1st BASE-3rd BASE
RED SOX

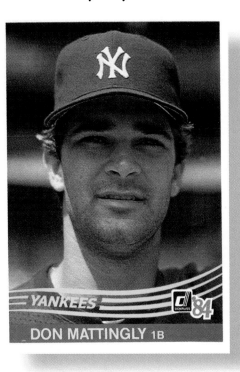

YANKEES
DON MATTINGLY 1B

1984 DONRUSS DON MATTINGLY #248

For a time during the 1980s and early '90s, this card was gold. It could have done just about anything for you, save for serving as a down payment on a car or paying off a credit card debt. But who knows? The folks at MasterCard just might have listened. Donnie Baseball and this card were both that hot. It was, and remains, the key card in the '84 Donruss set, famous for its design and shorter quantities of cards.

$15–$30

1984 FLEER UPDATE DWIGHT GOODEN #U43

Doc Gooden could, as the kids like to say, "bring it." At age 19 in 1984, Dr. K set records for most strikeouts by a rookie (276) and most strikeouts in consecutive games (32, having fanned 16 in consecutive starts). He also started the 1984 All-Star Game and whiffed the side in order in the first inning. To the suprise of no one, Gooden was the NL Rookie of the Year. This card, because Fleer drastically cut production of its Update set, was the card of choice to all collectors wanting the best Gooden card to own in '84.

$8–$15

Dwight Gooden
PITCHER

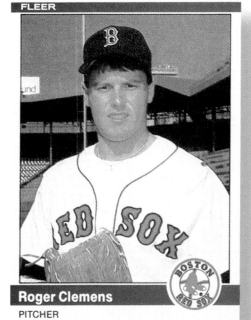

Roger Clemens
PITCHER

1984 FLEER UPDATE ROGER CLEMENS #U27

A tough, tough card of a tough, tough pitcher. Five Cy Young awards makes this first big-league Clemens card one of the most significant pitcher cards of the century and places him in the same breath with Ryan, Koufax and Gibson. The fact that Clemens wrapped up the century playing in New York for the Yankees only adds more gloss to this card, as if it ever needed it.

$175–$250

Kirby Puckett
OUTFIELD

1984 FLEER UPDATE KIRBY PUCKETT #U93

An eye ailment ended Puckett's career prematurely, but the barrel-shaped star will be remembered as maybe the best-hitting right-handed batter of his generation. Puckett could do it all: hit, hit for power, run the bases well and play a Gold Glove center field. He helped the Twins to two World Series championships, and should be entering the Hall of Fame in the very near future.

$60–$100

1985 TOPPS ROGER CLEMENS #181

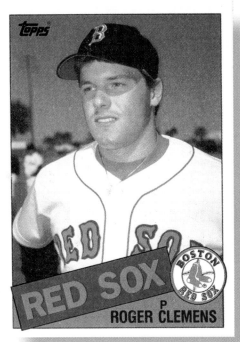

For many players with multiple Rookie Cards, the Fleer or Donruss RCs often are in more demand from collectors. Part of this comes from a perceived scarcity when compared to Topps cards from the mid-1980s. But here's a Topps card that is gaining some legitimacy as the Clemens RC to own. One reason might be that Fleer included Clemens in its 1984 Update set while Topps did not. So this card became the first Topps card of Clemens, and a key card to Topps collectors. A real competitor, Clemens was just beginning to make a name for himself at the time of this release.

$18–$30

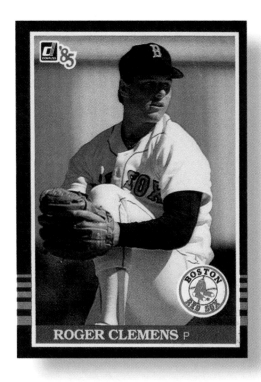

1985 DONRUSS ROGER CLEMENS #273

The Rocket in motion. A nice Rookie Card of a man who has recorded 20 strikeouts in a game twice and has (so far) won a record five Cy Young awards. Just watch those edges; they chip easily.

$30–$50

1985 DONRUSS TOM SEAVER (CORRECT) #424

Of all the errors on baseball cards over the years, this corrected card is linked to one of the strangest. Somehow, somebody at Donruss confused left-handed pitcher Floyd Bannister, a marginal player, with right-handed pitcher Tom Seaver, a first ballot Hall of Famer. How this happened is a mystery, but it happened. Donruss did correct the rather embarrassing goof, but only included the corrected card in 1985 factory sets. So it's entirely possible that someone, somewhere built a hand-collated 1985 set and is under the false impression that Tom Seaver is a big, hard-throwing left-hander.

$10–$20

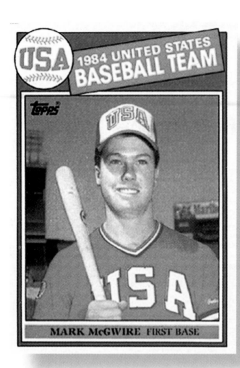

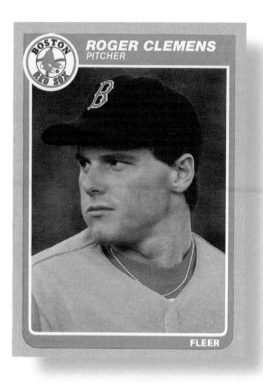

1985 TOPPS MARK McGWIRE #401

Before 1998, this was merely the Rookie Card of a solid home run hitter. By the end of '98, this was the Rookie Card of baseball's single-season home run king and was being hailed as a cornerstone to any collection. Funny what a 70-home-run season can do for a card.

$100–$200

1985 FLEER ROGER CLEMENS #155

Another Clemens Rookie Card, and perhaps the toughest one to find of the three. Centered copies are in real demand, but rarely seen.

$30–$50

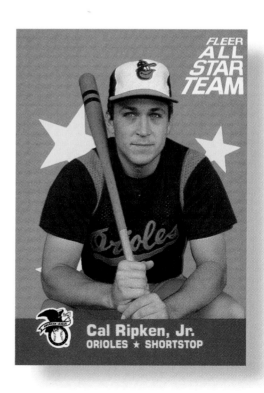

1986 FLEER ALL-STARS CAL RIPKEN JR. #5

Although the idea of inserts didn't originate with Fleer, the company did raise the bar in 1986 when it randomly inserted 12 different All-Star cards in wax and cello packs. Collectors loved the idea, and the cards were good looking to boot. The Ripken card remains the best of the set.

$5–$12

1986 DONRUSS JOSE CANSECO #39

Some cards are hot before they're ever printed, which is really quite amazing when you think about it. In the case of this former Oakland A's Bash Brother, it was a .302 average and five home runs in 29 games during a late-season call-up in '85 that created a buzz for Canseco. Of course, becoming just the 27th player in major league history to blast a home run over the roof of 75-year-old Comisky Park — it's right there on his card back — will get a guy noticed, too. There was a time when this card was trading for triple figures on the market. Of course, there was also a time when a dealer would have been thrilled to get a $20 bill for one. Now it's somewhere in-between.

$30–$50

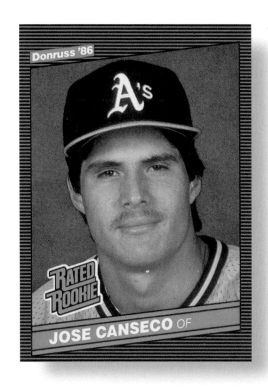

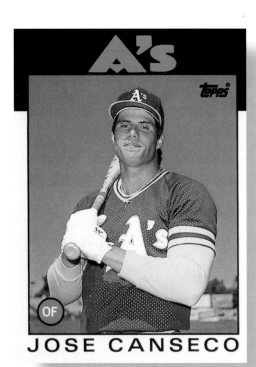

1986 TOPPS TRADED JOSE CANSECO #20T

In 1986, both Donruss and Fleer beat Topps to the punch in releasing a Jose Canseco card. Well, they did get him in the '86 Traded set and the Bash-Brother-to-be is one of the affordable cards that make the '86 Topps Traded set worth picking up.

$3–$6

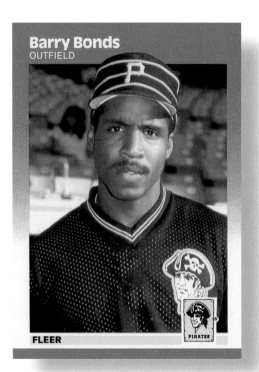

1987 FLEER BARRY BONDS #604

Bonds is the first member of the 400 home run/400 stolen bases club and has a shot at being the first to 500/500. Bonds is Willie Mays' godson, and someone who inherited Mays' baseball genes, even if it was by osmosis. The 1987 Fleer Bonds is a key card to own from the 1980s, and finding a clean card is difficult because of the solid blue border.

$25–$40

1987 DONRUSS MARK McGWIRE #46

Like quite a few other Mark McGwire cards, this second-year issue benefited greatly from the home run race of '98. What's amazing is that this card seemed to gain a life of its own overnight. For years it was little more than a good card of a good player, and there were plenty to be had. Then suddenly it's a great card of a great player, and everybody wants one. The baseball card game is much like the game of baseball itself, and the same principle applies. Mainly this: You never know.

$15–$30

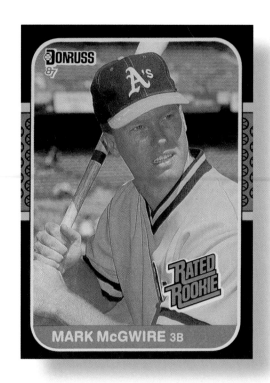

1987 FLEER UPDATE MARK McGWIRE #U76

When the price of 1985 Topps Mark McGwire Rookie Cards continued to climb during the Summer of '98, collectors started looking for other early McGwire cards to grab before the next guy did. This was one that held little interest until the home runs started leaving NL ballparks by the dozens. Then this was a keeper.

$10–$20

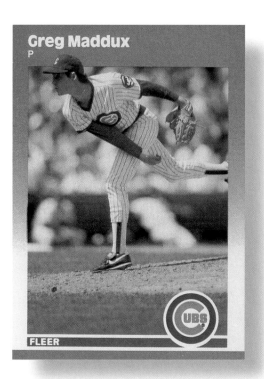

1987 FLEER UPDATE GREG MADDUX #U68

At the time of this card's release in a boxed set, Maddux was 6–14 with a 5.61 ERA for the Chicago Cubs. Obviously, things got better. At least for Maddux.

$6–$12

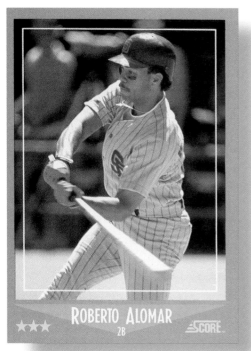

Before the unfortunate spitting incident with home plate umpire John Hirshbeck, Robby Alomar possessed a nearly flawless reputation as a ballplayer and person. And it was well deserved. He signed autographs by the dozens, smiled at the fans, waved, and performed amazing feats at second base. So it was no wonder that collectors were all over this card shortly after its release with the Rookie and Traded boxed set. The set just happened to turn out to be the shortest-printed update set of all time. After stints with the Padres, Blue Jays and Orioles, Alomar is now the second baseman of the Cleveland Indians and enjoying a resurgence in his career. Have the fans finally forgiven him? Maybe. After softening significantly in recent seasons, this card is again picking up interest among collectors.

$9–$15

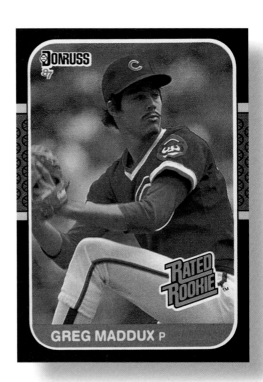

1987 DONRUSS GREG MADDUX #36

Maddux, with four Cy Young awards to his name, has been the NL's most dominant pitcher of the '90s. He's changed uniforms and lost the little pencil-thin mustache since this Rookie Card was released. Centered copies of this black-bordered gem are as rare as a player getting a three-hit game against the Atlanta ace.

$13–$25

1989 DONRUSS KEN GRIFFEY JR. #33

Dark borders and difficult centering on this card make it a challenge to find in top condition. Like the '89 Fleer Griffey Jr. RC, this Donruss issue just recently caught the attention of the collecting public. Junior's home run outbursts certainly have had something to do with that, as has the rise in professionally graded card services which see plenty of this card pass through.

$13–$25

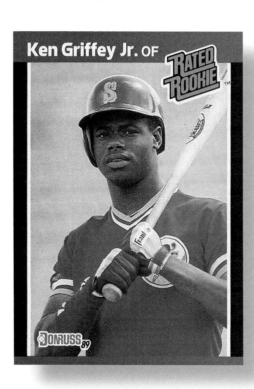

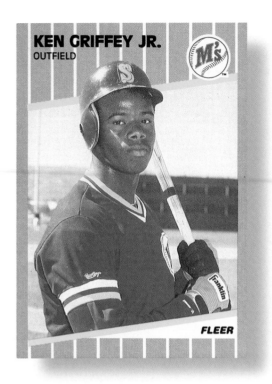

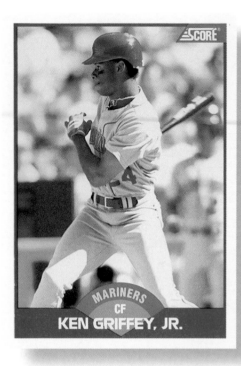

1989 FLEER KEN GRIFFEY JR. #548

For several years this card seemed to be underappreciated by collectors. Maybe it was just lost in the shadow of the '89 Upper Deck Griffey. But that's all changed. This card is now seen, and appreciated, for what it is — a Rookie Card of today's best player.

$13–$25

1989 SCORE ROOKIE/TRADED KEN GRIFFEY JR. #100T

One of the more glaring mistakes Score made early in 1989 was leaving Ken Griffey Jr. out of its regular set. If you wanted a card of Junior, you either bought Donruss, Fleer or Upper Deck. (Topps didn't get him in until its late-season Traded set.) But Score rallied in the late innings and produced a reasonably smaller print run of Rookie/Traded sets, including Griffey Jr. A most wise decision, indeed.

$30–$45

1989 DONRUSS BASEBALL'S BEST SAMMY SOSA #324

Thanks to Donruss, we remember Sammy as a Ranger. We're quite sure Texas fans would like to have Sammy back, but hey, some deals just explode in your face. This card lay dormant until Sosa went on a home run tear in 1998. It stands as the only major league card of Sosa issued in '89.

$10–$20

1989 UPPER DECK KEN GRIFFEY JR. #1

Talk about making the right call; Upper Deck chose Junior to kick off its debut set, a premium issue like no other before it. Great move. The card is arguably among the most important baseball releases of the century, and its future still looks as bright as the player who graces the card front. For all its technology and special releases, this remains the true gem of The Upper Deck Company.

Ken Griffey Jr.

$100–$160

Randy Johnson

1989 UPPER DECK RANDY JOHNSON #25

Yes, there really was a time when The Big Unit (Le Unite Gros) was operating north of the border in French-speaking Montreal.

$3–$6

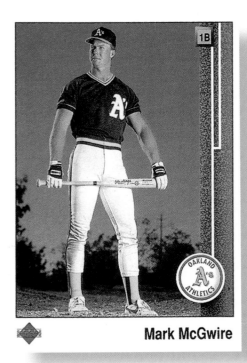

Mark McGwire

1989 UPPER DECK MARK McGWIRE #300

Big Mac, standing tall exactly 10 years before towering over everyone who's ever played the game.

$2–$5

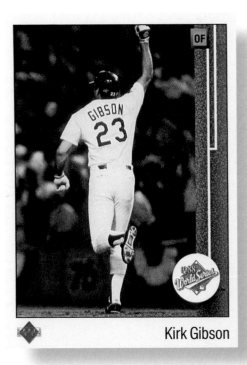

Kirk Gibson

1989 UPPER DECK WORLD SERIES (KIRK GIBSON) #666

Time stands still in this memorable shot.

50 cents–$1

NOLAN RYAN

he decade opened with the release of another premium set, this one produced by Donruss and called Leaf. The hook with 1990 Leaf was production; the cards were produced in fewer quantities than Donruss' competitors, and featured a hot Frank Thomas Rookie Card as well as a second-year card of Ken Griffey Jr.

Leaf was the exception in the early '90s. Other sets were produced in mass quantities and shipped to collectors. Inserts became the rage, as did technology. Terms such as die-cut, refractor and peel-off coating became common. Autographs began appearing on cards inserted in packs, and by the late '90s, some brands featured one autographed card per pack.

On the field, the major leagues welcomed the Florida Marlins, Colorado Rockies, Arizona Diamondbacks and Tampa Bay Devil Rays, Nolan Ryan pitched a sixth and seventh no-hitter, the Atlanta Braves, Toronto Blue Jays and Marlins all captured their first world championships and manager Joe Torre helped lead the New York Yankees back to prominence.

Baseball also endured a bitter 234-day player strike that wiped out the 1994 World Series — the first World Series not played since 1904. Once the players returned to the fields the following April, it took some time for the game to heal, but that was helped tremen-

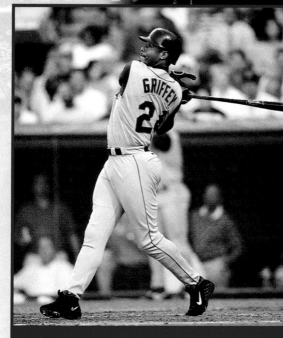

KEN GRIFFEY JR.

CAMDEN YARDS

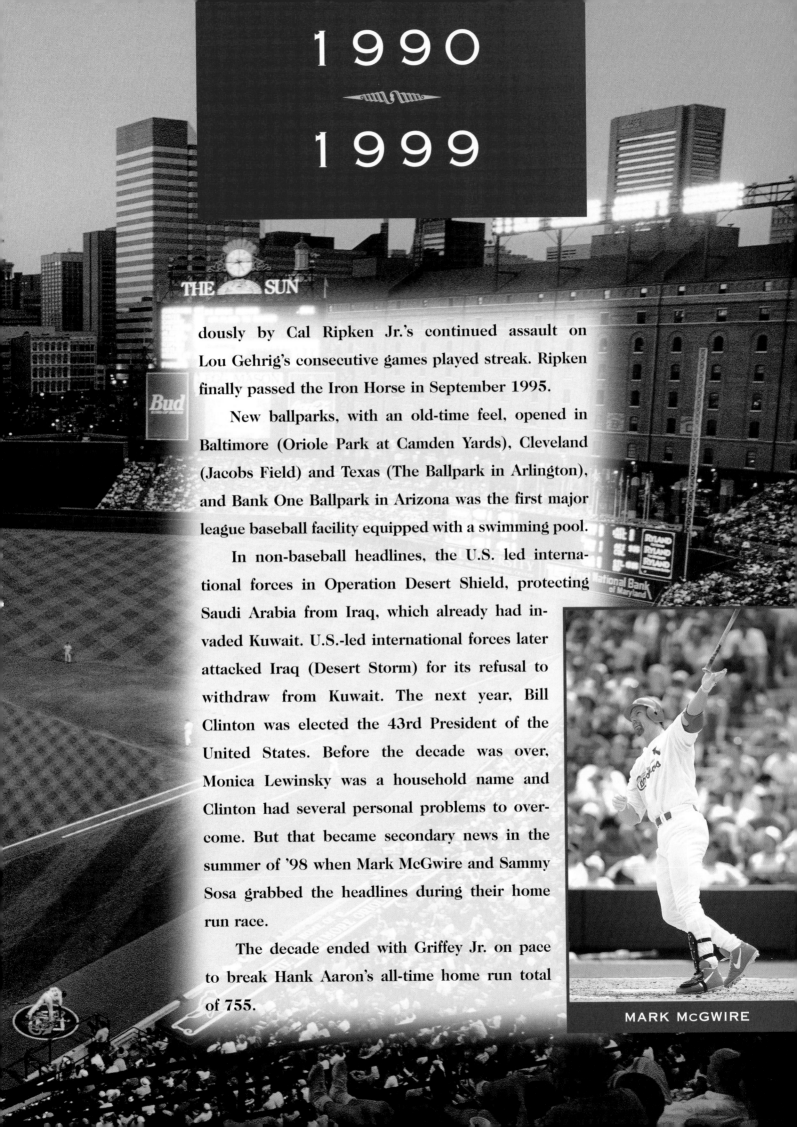

dously by Cal Ripken Jr.'s continued assault on Lou Gehrig's consecutive games played streak. Ripken finally passed the Iron Horse in September 1995.

New ballparks, with an old-time feel, opened in Baltimore (Oriole Park at Camden Yards), Cleveland (Jacobs Field) and Texas (The Ballpark in Arlington), and Bank One Ballpark in Arizona was the first major league baseball facility equipped with a swimming pool.

In non-baseball headlines, the U.S. led international forces in Operation Desert Shield, protecting Saudi Arabia from Iraq, which already had invaded Kuwait. U.S.-led international forces later attacked Iraq (Desert Storm) for its refusal to withdraw from Kuwait. The next year, Bill Clinton was elected the 43rd President of the United States. Before the decade was over, Monica Lewinsky was a household name and Clinton had several personal problems to overcome. But that became secondary news in the summer of '98 when Mark McGwire and Sammy Sosa grabbed the headlines during their home run race.

The decade ended with Griffey Jr. on pace to break Hank Aaron's all-time home run total of 755.

MARK McGWIRE

1990 SCORE BO JACKSON #697

Bo knew two sports during his brief baseball/football career, and collectors loved him. As an outfielder with the Kansas City Royals, his play on the ball field resembled the inconsistent golf games of so many of us: strikeout, weak hit, mammoth home run. The only thing you knew for sure with Bo was that you didn't want to be making a hot dog run when he was stepping to the plate. A 500-foot blast could be just one swing away. This card was the darling of collectors upon its release. Collectors piecing together sets of Score were led to believe — probably from other misinformed collectors — that this card was short-printed by the company. It wasn't. Instead, it was just extremely popular. Just like Bo himself.

20 cents–50 cents

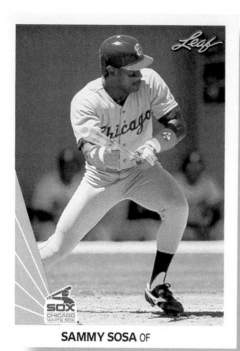

SAMMY SOSA OF

FRANK THOMAS 1B

1990 LEAF SAMMY SOSA #220

In a matter of a few months during the 1998 season, this card was getting as much publicity within the hobby community as the 1985 Topps Mark McGwire card. While Sosa was chasing Maris and McGwire during the great home run race of '98, collectors were pulling this card out of commons and semi-stars boxes where it had resided for years. And with each shot Sammy sent into the night, those same collectors looked at this card and saw Slammin' Sammy . . . bunting.

$35–$60

1990 LEAF FRANK THOMAS #300

On the heels of 1989 Upper Deck came 1990 Leaf, another "premium" release, although one produced in lesser quantities than the '89 UD set. The card that led the way from the first day of release was Frank Thomas. Almost from the outset collectors knew The Big Hurt was The Big Deal, and his Rookie Card helped fuel sales of '90 Leaf Series II.

$35–$60

1990 Upper Deck Reggie Jackson Autograph #AU1

The concept of autographed cards inserted into baseball packs can be traced to high-number packs of '90 Upper Deck, which included 2,500 personally signed Reggie Jackson autographed Heroes cards. Back in 1990, this made headlines and set a precedent for the way the card hobby does business today.

$75–$125

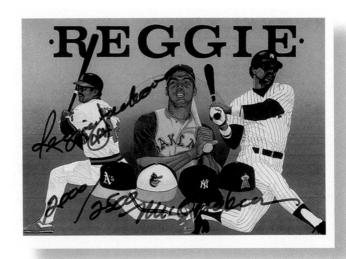

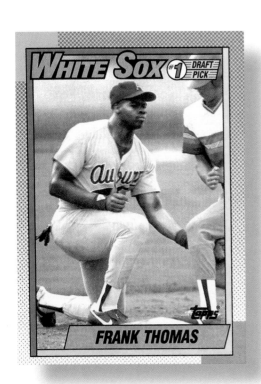

1990 Topps Frank Thomas #414

It's just a matter of time before baseball's second Frank Thomas eclipses the first Frank Thomas (a three-time National League All-Star in the '50s) in production. This Thomas — The Big Hurt — was just coming up to the big leagues when this readily available card was included in 1990 Topps packs. The photo is from Thomas' college days at Auburn, but check out the faceless (airbrushed?) base runner getting back to first base. What happened to his face?!

$2–$4

1991 Stadium Club Jeff Bagwell #388

Deals, unfortunately, are a lot like marriages: some work fabulously, and both parties are pleased for eternity; others look good at the start, then fade quickly. In 1990, the Boston Red Sox needed a quick fix in the bullpen. And they got it, acquiring relief pitcher Larry Andersen for minor league third baseman Jeff Bagwell. While Bagwell was a local New England kid, the Red Sox believed the deal was the right one to meet the immediate needs of the ballclub. Besides, Boston had Wade Boggs at third base. He was going to spend his entire career in Beantown, right? Bagwell, as we know, has gone on to bigger and better things in Houston, including winning an MVP Award. Both Boggs and Andersen are long gone from Boston. For Red Sox fans left wondering what might have been, the honeymoon is clearly over.

$2–$5

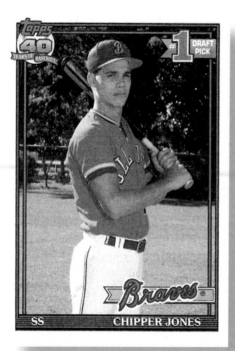

1991 TOPPS CHIPPER JONES #333

Chipper in a photo taken while a high school student at The Bolles School in Jacksonville, Fla., back in the days when the most important things in life were passing Algebra, getting a decent fitting uniform and putting solid aluminum on the ball. Things were so much easier then.

$3–$6

1991 BOWMAN IVAN RODRIGUEZ #272

Even back in '91, on this Rookie Card, Pudge Rodriguez looked as if he was born to catch.

$2–$5

1991 BOWMAN CHIPPER JONES #569

The Atlanta Braves had a real dilemma on their hands. With a history of losing seasons since their arrival in Atlanta from Milwaukee in 1966, the Braves had the first pick in the 1990 amateur draft and could not afford to blow it. The pick had to be a sure thing, someone who could come in and help anchor the Braves' climb to respectability, and, according to the blueprint, into elite status in the National League. And the Braves thought they had their man in high schooler Todd Van Poppel, a prospect all clubs coveted. But Van Poppel balked at the prospect of the Braves, or anyone, drafting him, and voiced his intention to attend the University of Texas. And so the Braves did the safe thing and passed on Van Poppel. Alas, Van Poppel was drafted in the first round and signed by the Athletics. The Braves? They "settled" for another high schooler: Larry "Chipper" Jones. Jones signed with the Braves, and the rest, as they say, is history.

$8–$15

1991 ULTRA UPDATE JUAN GONZALEZ #55

The proliferation of regular issue sets in the early '90s meant that many superstar players had Rookie Cards produced in sizeable quantities. Juan Gonzalez is one of those players: great athlete, really common Rookie Cards. But a year after his RCs were released, Fleer slipped Juando into its first-ever Ultra Update set, giving the two-time AL MVP his most valuable early-career card of all.

$15–$30

JUAN GONZALEZ — RANGERS OUTFIELD

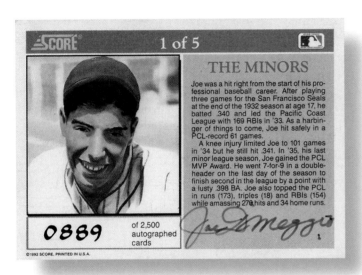

SCORE — 1 of 5

THE MINORS

Joe was a hit right from the start of his professional baseball career. After playing three games for the San Francisco Seals at the end of the 1932 season at age 17, he batted .340 and led the Pacific Coast League with 169 RBIs in '33. As a harbinger of things to come, Joe hit safely in a PCL-record 61 games.

A knee injury limited Joe to 101 games in '34 but he still hit .341. In '35, his last minor league season, Joe gained the PCL MVP Award. He went 7-for-9 in a doubleheader on the last day of the season to finish second in the league by a point with a lusty .398 BA. Joe also topped the PCL in runs (173), triples (18) and RBIs (154) while amassing 270 hits and 34 home runs.

0889 — of 2,500 autographed cards

©1992 SCORE, PRINTED IN U.S.A.

1992 SCORE JOE DiMAGGIO AUTOGRAPH

There might never have been a set as abundantly produced as 1992 Score Baseball. It was everywhere, and you could get it in any quantity. Someone once joked that the entire tap water supply of North America would run out before '92 Score did, which, quite frankly, might have been true. But while the presses rolled, so did the assembly line of collectors furiously ripping open Series I packs in hopes of finding a Joe DiMaggio autographed card. Score had inserted 2,500 DiMaggio autographs in Series I packs, and for many of us, it was like trying to find the golden needle in the haystack. Only this haystack was very, very large. And very, very abundant.

$300–$500

1992 TOPPS TRADED NOMAR GARCIAPARRA #39T

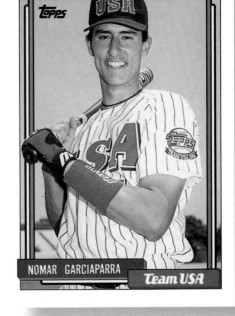

NOMAR GARCIAPARRA — Team USA

Who could have known? Other than the United States Olympic Team, and, of course, Topps, who could have figured that Garciaparra would develop into the dangerous hitter he is today? The only way collectors could get this card was through the Topps Traded boxed set released later in '92 — a set that contained cards of Team USA players. From the Fall of '98 to Spring of '99, this card doubled in value and reached triple figures. Who could have known?

$65–$100

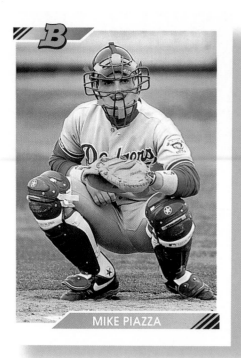

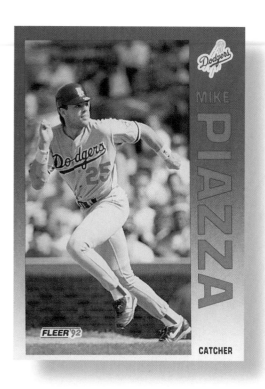

1992 FLEER UPDATE MIKE PIAZZA #92

Is that skinny kid running the bases really *the* Mike Piazza? Indeed it is. Before the bulk, fu manchu and familiar uniform #31 came onto the scene, Piazza was just another skinny kid looking for a chance to stick in Tinsel Town. Because this card was issued only in complete set form, and Fleer's orders weren't exceptionally large and thus they didn't overproduce the set, this ranks as the toughest major-league Piazza card to find.

$70–$100

1992 BOWMAN MIKE PIAZZA #461

It really wasn't supposed to work out the way it did. The Dodgers, with their pick in the 62nd round of the 1988 amateur draft — the 62nd round! — were just doing manager Tommy Lasorda a favor by selecting Lasorda family friend Michael Piazza. Then the Piazza boy began playing like anything but a late-round pick, and before anyone really knew it, the kid was in Los Angeles catching the likes of Orel Hershiser and Tim Belcher, and lighting up the place. The 62nd rounder had made it, as had his Bowman card, the kid's first big-league card out of the chute.

$35–$60

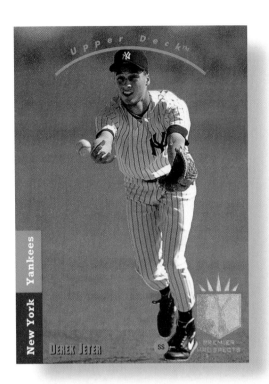

1993 SP DEREK JETER #279

One of baseball's best all-around short-stops also is featured on one of the most condition-sensitive cards produced in the 1990s. Chipping around the foil corners of this card is common. Finding one that is 100 percent problem free, ain't-no-smudges-or-marks-on-this-baby Gem Mint is as tough as trying to blow a fastball by Jeter while you're down in the count. Good luck.

$55–$80

1994 SP ALEX RODRIGUEZ #15

As we approach the millennium, three current shortstops continue to raise the position to one of power and grace. Like Cal Ripken before them, Nomar Garciaparra, Derek Jeter and Alex Rodriguez are sluggers capable of hitting the long ball just as easily as turning two to get out of an inning. But while Nomar and Jeter were both pictured on Topps cards early in their professional careers, A-Rod was not, due to a dispute he had with the cardmaker over rights to his likeness. So while Topps went without Rodriguez for several seasons (the two finally patched up their differences for the '98 set), Rodriguez went without a Rookie Card until he reached the majors. In 1994, this foil card, susceptible to chipping and damage, was released of the then 19-year-old phenom.

$50–$80

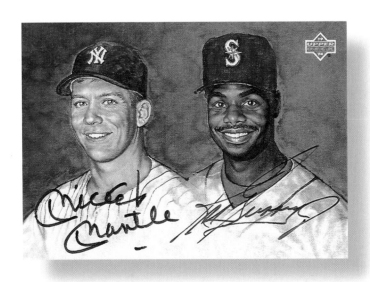

1994 UPPER DECK KEN GRIFFEY JR./MICKEY MANTLE AUTOGRAPH #GM1

Upper Deck really had it going on in '94, having baseball stars such as Griffey and Mantle signed to contracts to promote their products and sign autographs. And UD utilized its resources wisely, having both players sign 1,000 of the same card to be inserted into packs. This card clearly stands as one of the greatest dual-signed cards in hobby history.

$800–$1,200

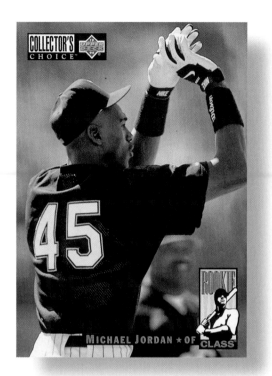

1994 COLLECTOR'S CHOICE MICHAEL JORDAN #661

This guy had a shooter's touch from anywhere. Even the baseball diamond.

$3–$5

1996 LEAF SIGNATURE SERIES EXTENDED SAMMY SOSA AUTOGRAPH

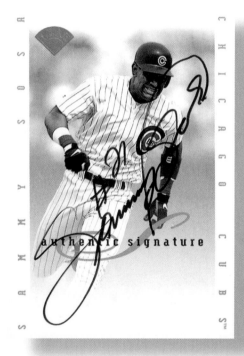

Just two years before he became a household name, Sammy could be found in this one-autograph-per-pack series. It wasn't until he was wrapped up in the home run race of '98 that many collectors realized that, of all the autographed inserts covering all brands in recent years, this was the only one Sosa appeared on. Almost overnight, this became a key card of a key player.

$90–$150

1996 TOPPS MICKEY MANTLE #7

No other card manufacturer captured the spirit of Mickey Mantle better than Topps, from the '52 Topps to the '69 card issued after his final season on the field. In 1996, with history on its side, Topps released reprints of the entire Mantle Topps library, including in its regular set this card to honor Mantle, who had died a year earlier. As a final tip of the cap to the man who helped shape baseball and the baseball card hobby, Topps announced that card #7 from all future issues would be retired. This is the last #7 in Topps' baseball history.

$2–$4

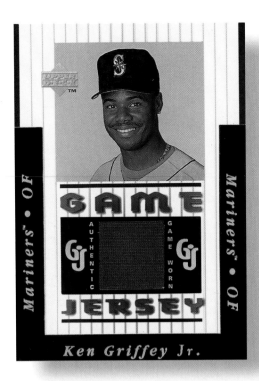

1997 UPPER DECK GAME JERSEY KEN GRIFFEY JR. #GJ1

About one in every 800 packs of 1997 Upper Deck's 1st Series yielded one of three cards carrying a swatch of an actual game-worn jersey. The player selection consisted of three players: future Hall of Famer Tony Gwynn, HOFer-in-the-making Ken Griffey Jr. and Rey Ordonez, a fine player but one who currently is on nobody's future HOFer list. But it was Griffey, Upper Deck's spokesman, who attracted the most collector attention, especially after a home run barrage during the season that saw Junior seriously threaten Roger Maris' single-season home run mark and cement his place in current baseball lore.

$350–$600

1999 UPPER DECK CENTURY'S LEGENDS 500 CLUB JIMMIE FOXX GAME-USED BAT

Some 54 years after his last game, the bat of Double X is still just as powerful today as it was while he was hitting his 534 career home runs. This is a great card, allowing collectors of today to gain an appreciation for Foxx, one of the game's truly great power hitters.

$175–$350

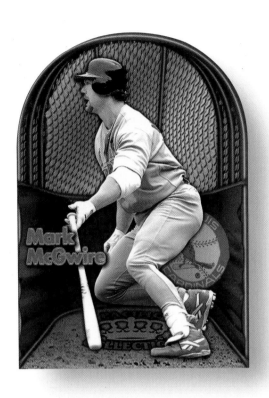

1998 PACIFIC "IN THE CAGE" MARK McGWIRE #13

The Pacific Trading Card Company took die-cutting to another level — actually maybe two levels — with these In The Cage inserts. The intricate cutting of the net is outstanding, allowing the holder to see through the netting and bringing a uniqueness to the card. This Mark McGwire card is the most valuable of the 20-card set.

$40–$100

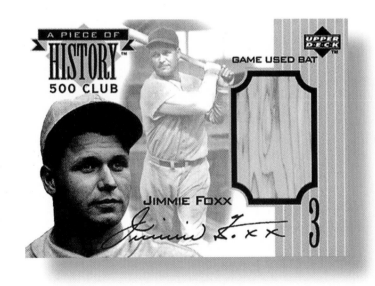

1999 UPPER DECK A PIECE OF HISTORY BABE RUTH GAME-USED BAT

The final year in the millennium yielded one of the most innovative cards ever, a card carrying a slice of one of Babe Ruth's game-used bats. (A special cut autograph version, limited to three, also was produced.) Upper Deck was criticized by some baseball purists for cutting up such an important baseball artifact, but the company pointed out that several other Bambino gamers were still on the market, and that getting A Piece of History into collectors' hands was a good thing for everyone. Those who pulled the card from a pack or who bought one on the secondary market — or even those of us mere mortals who could only dream of such a windfall — tended to agree.

$750–$1,500

1999 TOPPS MARK MCGWIRE #220 (HOME RUN #70)

Topps had 70 reasons to love Mark McGwire as the '99 Series I cards went to press. The venerable card manufacturer printed card #220 in the set with 70 different variations, and it didn't take long for the collecting frenzy to begin. All 70 cards carry the same picture on the front, but each card features a different home run number. Card backs do differ, with the text highlighting that card's particular home run. The #70 home run card ultimately became collectors' primary target, and at one point confirmed sales figures reached triple figures, which, the optimist will point out, is still cheaper than the #70 ball.

$75–$125